WADSWORTH PHILOSOPHERS SERIES

ON

ARENDT

Patricia Altenbernd Johnson
University of Dayton

WADSWORTH

TM

THOMSON LEARNING

Australia • Canada • Mexico • Singapore • Spain
United Kingdom • United States

Printed in the United States of America
2 3 4 5 6 7 04 03 02 01

For permission to use material from this text, contact us:
Web: http://www.thomsonrights.com
Fax: 1-800-730-2215
Phone: 1-800-730-2214

For more information, contact:
Wadsworth Thomson Learning, Inc.
10 Davis Drive
Belmont, CA 94002-3098
USA
http://www.wadsworth.com

ISBN: 0-534-58361-X

Contents

1

Between Birth and Death

Hannah Arendt wrote to her teacher and friend, Karl Jaspers, in July of 1926, "I try to interpret history, try to understand what is expressed in it, from the perspective that I have gained through my own experience" (Letter 1). Her experience led her to the conviction that although all humans must die, each is born to begin. In *The Human Condition* she writes,

> *If left to themselves, human affairs can only follow the law of mortality, which is the most certain and the only reliable law of a life spent between birth and death. It is the faculty of action that interferes with this law....* (246)

This faculty of action enables humans to interrupt life and to begin new projects. Interpreting life through the perspective of this insight provided Arendt with hope in dark times and with the capability of beginning her life again in new situations and new places.

Beginning Life in Germany

Hannah Arendt began life on October 14, 1906. Her parents, Paul and Martha Arendt, named her Johanna, but she was always known simply as Hannah. While she was born into a very loving family, she experienced deep sorrow and disruption at a very early age.

Königsberg

The Arendts were both from Jewish families who had established themselves in Königsberg, East Prussia. When Hannah was three, the family returned to Königsberg because her father was ill with syphilis. He was hospitalized in 1911 and died in 1913. That same year, Max Arendt, Hannah's grandfather also died. In August of 1914, Martha Arendt fled with Hannah to Berlin to escape the threat of Russian invasion. However, they were able to return to Königsberg that same year and lived through World War I in relative stability. Martha Arendt took in lodgers and depended on her family for financial assistance. Hannah suffered a period of illness that was probably precipitated by the deaths of her father and grandfather. However, she was finally able to settle into school. The challenge of learning and thinking provided her with one of her earliest experiences of the power of beginnings. Her health improved and she began to thrive.

Hannah also began to experience the importance of the political at this point in her life. Martha Arendt opened her home to social democrats and participated in a discussion group on political issues. While she was generally opposed to the Spartacists, the revolutionary communist group led by Rosa Luxemburg, she was an admirer of Luxemburg herself. In 1919, she supported the general strike led by the Spartacists. Elizabeth Young-Bruehl, author of the most thorough biography of Hannah Arendt, reports that Martha admonished her daughter to remember that she was experiencing an historical moment (28). While the revolution failed, Martha Arendt continued her participation in the political issues that faced Germany.

In February of 1920, Martha Arendt married Martin Beerwald, a widower with two daughters, Eva and Clara. Martha and Hannah moved to the Beerwald home, and the two families worked at developing a union. Hannah, however, never fully embraced this union, and often preferred to go her own way. She began smoking, a habit that would remain with her for life, and formed a "Greek Circle." Friends joined her in her room in the Beerwald home to read and discuss Greek classics. She began reading Kierkegaard and Kant, and she wrote poetry that expressed her emotional ambiguities. In one poem, that she titles "Weariness," she writes,

2

What I have loved
I cannot hold.
What lies around me
I cannot leave.

Everything declines
While darkness rises.
Nothing overcomes me—
This must be life's way. (Young-Bruehl 37)

Her intellectual growth was beginning and her years at University between 1924 and 1929 provided her with the opportunity to study with some of the most exciting scholars of the twentieth century.

University Experience

At the age of eighteen, Hannah Arendt went to Marburg to study with the theologian Rudolf Bultmann and the philosophers Nicolai Hartmann and Martin Heidegger. Heidegger was in the process of working out the thought for his major work, *Being and Time.* Arendt attended his lectures and was profoundly influenced by Heidegger's exciting new approach to philosophy. While her own work eventually parted with Heidegger's, her thought was fundamentally shaped by this Marburg experience.

Heidegger was married, had two children, and was thirty-five years old when Arendt arrived in Marburg. He had had some difficulty in obtaining a University position and was just beginning to establish his philosophical reputation. Arendt was both inspired by Heidegger's thought and attracted to him as a man. Heidegger initiated an affair that could have cost him his position and his marriage. They quickly realized that the affair could not continue, and ended it in 1925, although Arendt remained in contact with Heidegger for several more years and resumed a friendly contact after the end of World War II. When the friendship resumed, Heidegger told Arendt that she was the inspiration for much of his thought. In 1925, however, they agreed to remain silent about the affair, and she left to study first at Freiburg and then in Heidelberg.

In Heidelberg she studied with Karl Jaspers. He was to remain her mentor and friend for the rest of her life. Jaspers, like Heidegger, developed existentialist philosophy. He moved into philosophy from

3

psychology and was more concerned with interpersonal relations than Heidegger was. He did not have the same intellectual influence on Arendt as did Heidegger, but he modeled for her the sort of life that she came to recognize as characterized by thinking. Under Jasper's supervision, she wrote a dissertation on *The Concept of Love in Augustine.*

During this period she renewed and deepened a friendship with Hans Jonas, a fellow student whom she had known in Marburg. This friendship, like that with Jaspers, lasted for the rest of her life. She also renewed her acquaintance with Günther Stern, whom she knew from her days in Marburg. They soon began living together, and in September of 1929, they married. Stern helped her with editing the final draft of her dissertation. When it was completed, they moved to Frankfort so that Stern could pursue work towards his *Habilitation*. In the German academic system, this work includes lecturing and writing that are preliminary to receiving an appointment to a University faculty.

The Frankfurt Experience and a Move to Berlin

Stern was working on a project in the philosophy of music and hoped to be able to lecture at Frankfurt because of its growing reputation as a vital intellectual community. Paul Tillich, the theologian, was at Frankfurt, and both Stern and Arendt attended his lectures. This was the period during which a group of young Marxist thinkers founded the Institute for Social Research, which was to become known as The Frankfurt School. While neither Stern nor Arendt was Marxist, they engaged in philosophical exchanges with these thinkers, and Arendt became increasingly interested in political issues. Max Horkheimer, Herbert Marcuse, and Theodor Adorno were all part of the group. When Stern submitted his work on philosophy of music, Adorno, who wrote in the field and who was the primary reader for the work, rejected it.

Nazi influence was also increasing, and Stern realized that anti-Semitism in the universities, in addition to the rejection of his philosophical work, would make it practically impossible for him to gain a teaching position. He and Arendt decided to move to Berlin. Stern became a journalist and took the pseudonym that he would retain for his entire writing career, Günther Anders.

In Berlin, Arendt began work on a biography of Rahel Varnhagen and also renewed acquaintance with Kurt Blumenfeld. Blumenfeld had been a friend of her grandfather and was also an active Zionist. Both of these events led her to think seriously about what it meant for her to be Jewish, particularly in Germany.

The biography, *Rahel Varnhagen: The Life of a Jewish Woman*, was not printed until 1958, but most of the writing was done in 1932 and 1933 in Berlin. Varnhagen, born Rahel Levin in 1771, was a member of a well-situated Jewish family in Berlin. In her youth she conducted intellectual salons in the attic of her home. After the Napoleonic wars and the rise of anti-Semitism, she converted to Christianity and married August Varnhagen, a Christian man who was considerably younger than she. Rahel Varnhagen kept diaries and wrote introspective letters that revealed her struggles with her Jewish identity. In the end, she embraced that identity.

Arendt's account of Varnhagen's life is read by many as autobiography as much as biography. Arendt used the writing of the book to struggle with her own identity as a Jew in a period in which anti-Semitism was again threatening the German Jews. Influenced by Blumenfeld and other Zionists, Arendt does not simply write a biography, she engages in reflections on the ambiguities inherent in claiming both a German and a Jewish identity. Over a six-day period in January of 1933, Arendt and Jaspers corresponded on this issue. She writes to Jaspers that she thinks that for her to be German is to speak the language and read the philosophy and literature. He writes back to her, "How tricky this business with the German character is! I find it odd that you as a Jew want to set yourself apart from what is German" (Letter 23). He suggests to her that she needs to add a political and historical sense of destiny to her understanding of what it is to be German. Her reply to him is revealing. Her work on Varnhagen, done in the context of anti-Semitism and growing Zionism, has clearly led her to important insights about her own identity. She writes to Jaspers,

> *I am of course a German in the sense that I wrote of before. But I cannot simply add a German historical and political destiny to that. I know only too well how late and how fragmentary the Jew's participation in that destiny has been, how much by chance they entered into what was then a foreign history.... What my Germany is can hardly be expressed in one phrase, for any oversimplification – whether it is that of the Zionists, the assimilationists, of the anti-Semites – only serves to obscure the true problem of the situation.* (Letter 24)

Arendt does not join any of the groups that she lists. Like Varnhagen, she determines to be what she calls a 'conscious pariah.' She will not assimilate to the German culture, but will consciously live her identity as a social outsider.

Arendt's relationship with Stern became distant during the period in which they were in Berlin. She kept her thinking from him, sharing her thoughts more openly with people like Blumenfeld. In February of 1933, after the Reichstag was burned, Stern knew that his name was in an address book of leftist sympathizers that was probably in the hands of the Gestapo. He decided to leave Germany. Arendt chose to remain in Berlin and to work with Blumenfeld.

Because she was not a member of the Zionist organization she was able to do research on anti-Semitism in the Prussian State Library. She also provided refuge in her home for Communists who were fleeing Germany. However, she was arrested and held for questioning for eight days. She and her mother, who was living with her at the time, decided that it was time for them to flee. They left Germany, crossing the Czech border illegally through a safe house that admitted people through the front door in Germany and allowed them to exit through the back door into Czechoslovakia.

France and the Importance of Jewish Identity

Arendt and her mother first took refuge in Geneva, but Martha decided that she needed to return to Königsberg to be with her husband. Arendt moved to Paris where she rejoined her husband, Günther Stern. She brought him the manuscript of a satire on Fascism that he had had to leave behind when he fled Berlin. It reportedly smelled of bacon because it had been hidden in a cloth with the smoked bacon (May 39). Arendt and Stern lived together and socialized with common friends in Paris from 1933 to 1936, and Arendt continued to use the name Stern for public purposes. However, they did not resume marital relations. Stern immigrated to the United States in 1936 and they were officially divorced in 1937.

Arendt, remaining in Paris, determined that she would work politically to assist Jewish people. She took seriously the distinction that she learned from Blumenfeld between a "socially ambitious parvenu" and a "politically conscious pariah." She recognized that the only choices open to her were to be absorbed into the culture or to be an outsider. She judged that the first choice was an illusion for Jewish people. What was important was to consciously be an outsider

6

(Young-Bruehl 120-122). Arendt's work in Paris allowed her to live as a conscious pariah.

Arendt first worked as a secretary for Agriculture et Artisanat, a group that trained young Jews in preparation for emigration to Palestine. When work with this organization ended, she found a position with Youth Aliyah, another group that worked to send Jewish children to Palestine. In addition to developing training programs that provided the children with the skills that they would need in Palestine, she helped children deal with the psychological stress of anti-Semitism and the ambiguities of their political and personal situations. In 1935, she traveled with a group of children to Haifa and also had opportunity to visit Greek and Roman ruins. This trip inspired her with loyalty for the newly emerging Jewish community in Palestine, but she also began to fear that a Jewish nationalism could destroy what was best about this political experiment.

Arendt made and renewed many friendships while in Paris. She met Bertolt Brecht, the poet and playwright, as well as the philosopher Jean Paul Sartre. Anne Mendelssohn, a friend from her youth in Königsberg, was there with her husband, Eric Weil, and Mendelssohn and Arendt renewed their deep friendship. Arendt met Walter Benjamin, a Jewish intellectual whose friendship meant a great deal to her. When she finally left France, she carried with her some of his manuscripts to be delivered to members of the Frankfurt School who had gone to the United States. Benjamin, like Stern, had been admonished by Adorno for not being appropriately Marxist. However, eventually Arendt gave Benjamin's manuscripts to Adorno for publication. She wrote a wonderful essay on Benjamin that is included in *Men in Dark Times*.

Heinrich Blücher was the most significant person that Arendt met in Paris. Blücher was a Communist who had fled Berlin in 1934. He was older than Arendt and had been a member of the Spartacists, the group with which Rosa Luxemburg was associated. He was one of the first of that group to become a Communist and had a long history of political activities. His education was not systematic, but he had experimented with writing songs, film criticism, and psychology. He was passionate about ideas and politics. He was not Jewish. Arendt met Blücher at a lecture in 1936, and they soon began living together.

Arendt and Blücher developed a circle of friends in Paris and opened their home as a place for conversation and exchange of thoughts. This characterized their relationship for the rest of their lives. They developed a circle of intellectuals who felt comfortable in coming to their home to exchange ideas and challenge each other to think more deeply no matter where they lived.

The exuberance of life in Paris was quickly silenced. Arendt's mother recognized in April of 1939 that it was time for her to leave Germany. She joined Arendt and Blücher in Paris. Shortly after her arrival, Blücher was interned as a male German. When he was released, Arendt's mother encouraged them to marry, although she was not as fond of Blücher as she had been of Stern. She believed, correctly, that they had a better chance of obtaining US visas if they were married. They married in 1940 and remained married until Blücher died in 1970.

The marriage was in January, and both were sent to internment camps in May of the same year. She was sent to Gurs, but obtained release papers the next month. Friends provided her with sanctuary in Montauban. But, she had no word of Blücher. Then, they met by chance on the street one day. Like her, he had been released from an internment camp when France fell to Germany. Martha Beerwald was able to join them, and all three began to work to obtain visas to go to the United States. Günther Stern facilitated the process from the American side of the Atlantic. Eventually Arendt and Blücher obtained visas, but Martha Beerwald's was delayed. Arendt and Blücher decided to go on to Lisbon without her when there was a relaxation in exits-permit policy. They waited three months for a ship to New York. Martha Beerwald managed to escape and sail on a ship that left just three weeks later.

Arendt's friend, Walter Benjamin, was not so fortunate. He had an emergency exit visa to the United States, secured by the members of the Frankfurt School who were already in the United States. He also had a Spanish transit permit, and decided to leave through Spain. When he arrived at the border, the transit permit was not accepted and he was turned back. He took his own life that night, but because of this, the border officials let his companions through the next day. The manuscripts that Arendt carried to the United States were Benjamin's final works. As they waited for the ship in Lisbon, they read Benjamin's "Theses on the Philosophy of History." Arendt later wrote a poem in Benjamin's memory,

Dusk will come again sometime.
Night will come down from the stars.
We will rest our outstretched arms
In the nearnesses, in the distances.

Out of the darkness sound softly

Small archaic melodies. Listening,
Let us wean ourselves away,
Let us at last break ranks.

Distant voices, sadnesses nearby,
Those are the voices and these the dead
whom we have sent as messengers
Ahead, to lead us into slumber. (Young-Bruehl 163)

Beginning Again in the United States

Arendt and Blücher immigrated to New York City, arriving in May of 1941. They rented two rooms in a house on West 95th Street and provided Martha Beerwald with one of these rooms when she arrived. They lived in these quarters for ten years.

Communicating in English

Upon her arrival in New York, she took Benjamin's manuscripts to Adorno, who with others from the Frankfurt School had established the New School for Social Research in New York. Eventually these manuscripts would be important for intellectual thought, but initially Adorno handled them poorly, and Arendt wished that she had not given them to him.

The most urgent task for Arendt was to learn English. Her mother reminded her that in Königsberg she had preferred to learn French, Greek, and Latin, rather than English. Now she would have to learn English. Arendt was hosted by a family in Massachusetts and quickly began to develop the ability to communicate in English. She was supposed to stay for two months, but found the situation difficult. Young-Bruehl notes that Arendt "became aware that she could dislike American social life while admiring American political life" (166). Blücher sent a telegram that her mother was ill, and Arendt returned to New York. Soon she found work writing for a German language publication, Aufbau, and arguing for the formation of a Jewish army to join in the fight against Hitler. She also argued that Palestine should be both a Jewish and an Arab state with equality for all citizens.

Blücher found learning English difficult and, at first, took a position with a company in New Jersey shoveling chemicals. Soon he was able to become a research assistant with the Committee for National Morale, a group that at first tried to encourage the United States to enter the war, and after 1941 published stories of the atrocities in Europe.

This was a difficult transition for both Arendt and Blücher. She found herself at odds with many of the Zionist positions, yet she wanted to work for the Jewish people. He was struggling to make use of his talents for public speaking and journalism in a new language. They found it difficult to believe that the Nazis were carrying out the Final Solution to the Jewish Question, genocide. Their way of coping with the difficulties of their situation was to begin to outline a book. This would eventually be *The Origins of Totalitarianism*.

Arendt began work as an editor for Schocken Books in New York and also began to write for the *Partisan Review*. She was concerned with European Jewish culture and how it could be preserved and reclaimed. In the course of this work, she met many of the people who would become important to her American experience, including the poet, Randall Jarrell, and Mary McCarthy with whom she established a long friendship that included correspondence written over a period of almost thirty years. She and Blücher began to establish a group of friends, many of them immigrants like themselves. The circle of friends became larger as Arendt and Blücher became important intellectual voices in the United States.

The Post-War Period

World War II ended. Finally, life was stable enough that Arendt could focus on writing *The Origins of Totalitarianism*. Between 1945 and 1949, this work was her primary project (See Chapter 2).

However, during those years, other events interrupted Arendt's writing. Martin Beerwald, Arendt's stepfather, died in 1942. In 1948, her mother decided to go to London to live with Eva Beerwald. On the ship across the Atlantic, Martha Beerwald died. Hannah Arendt grieved this death deeply. Yet, it also released her from the pressures of trying to please her mother and mediate between Blücher and her mother. During this period, Heinrich Blücher also entered into an affair with another woman. This affair hurt Arendt, but she resolved to stay with Blücher and together they resolved to be honest with each other about their relationships.

As she worked on the book, she also renewed old friendships in Europe, especially with Jaspers. She wrote to him in November of 1945, summarizing the years that they had been unable to communicate,

> *Since I've been in America – that is, since 1941 – I've become a kind of freelance writer, something between a historian and a political journalist. In the latter capacity I've focused primarily on questions of Jewish politics. I've written about the German question only when growing hatred toward Germany and increasing idiocy about it made it impossible to remain silent, especially if one is a Jew.* (Letter 31)

In 1949, she decided to visit Germany, in part to distance herself from Blücher and his affair. She visited Jaspers and his wife, who was Jewish, in Basel. She and Jaspers began working together and renewed their correspondence after this visit.

From Basel, she went to Freiburg where she sent Heidegger a note. He came to her hotel to see her. It was after that visit that he told his wife that Arendt had been the inspiration for his work. While Arendt knew that Heidegger had been in the Nazi party for a year, she continued to appreciate what was passionate and exciting in his thought, and renewed her friendship with him. After this visit, she reportedly kept a photograph of Heidegger on her desk in New York (May 77). She and Blücher read Heidegger's writings as they were published, and she even helped him with publication. Heidegger, however, was never able to recognize her intellectual abilities and always viewed her simply as his Muse.

Establishing a Home in the United States

In 1951, Arendt received United States citizenship and *The Origins of Totalitarianism* was published. She and Blücher moved to a larger apartment on Morningside Drive in New York City. Her career began to develop. In 1952, she returned to Europe to seek publishers for French and German editions of *The Origins of Totalitarianism*. During this trip, she was confident in Blücher's loyalty, and they wrote frequently.

Meanwhile, Blücher helped to develop a Common Course for Bard College that focused on great thinkers and dealt with political and social critique. While she was in Europe, she received a Guggenheim grant to begin work on a new book that was to be a critique of Marxism. She also began to receive invitations to lecture at American universities such as Princeton and Berkeley. The Princeton invitation was to present the Christian Gauss seminars. While some remarked at a woman being invited for this honor, she objected to being considered an exceptional woman. Her refusal to be the "parvenu" helped her to understand the problems with being treated as a special or exceptional woman. While never a convinced and active feminist, Arendt clearly recognized the importance of political equality for women.

Arendt lectured and wrote prolifically between 1952 and 1962. While the project on Marxism never emerged in one book, she published several books in political philosophy during this period: *The Human Condition* (See Chapter 3), *Between Past and Future*, and *On Revolution*.

In 1958, Arendt was invited to give the Frankfurt Peace Prize address when the prize was given to Karl Jaspers for his book, *The Atom Bomb and the Future of Mankind*. Arendt was hesitant, afraid of speaking about Jaspers in public and afraid of antagonizing Heidegger by doing so. Blücher convinced her that it was important for her to take this opportunity to speak and to honor her friend in public for the character that he had demonstrated in such difficult times. Jaspers' wrote to her after the event,

> *In your words I saw reflected the deepest impulses of my life – indirectly, despite all your brilliant formulations – and in such a way that I feel confirmed and encouraged. It's strange: can we say things in public that we are reluctant to say in private? Does the public arena have a hidden aspect that can assume visible form only in public, an aspect that is comprehensible despite its not being explicit?* (Letter 232)

The address did distance Arendt from Heidegger, but it also enabled her to declare her intellectual independence. She sent him a copy of *The Human Condition* and so demonstrated to him her ability to be much more than his Muse.

Reflections on American Education

In *The Human Condition*, Arendt developed an analysis of human

12

life that makes use of three categories: private, social, and public. She used this theory as the theoretical background for an article, "Reflections on Little Rock." This article was initially commissioned for *Commentary*, a Jewish publication. However, when the editors read her article, they were very reluctant to print it. They commissioned Sidney Hook to write a reply. Even in this context, they hesitated to print Arendt's analysis of the racial situation in the schools. Arendt finally gave the article to another publication, *Dissent*. It appeared in the Winter 1959 issue, accompanied by two replies and a critical letter from Sidney Hook.

Arendt made use of her own childhood experience as a Jew, and so as an outsider in society, as well as the theoretical framework of *The Human Condition*, to reflect on the legally mandated integration of public schools. She was deeply moved by a photograph in *Life* that showed a young girl, part of the group that was integrating the Little Rock school system, being escorted home while white children shouted taunts at her. Arendt's article argued for the accomplishment of integration in the United State in areas that concerned adults rather than children. She fully believed in the equality of all humans, regardless of skin color or racial designation. However, she held that children should not be asked or expected to fight these battles. Indeed, she maintained that the parents of these children were exploiting them. She suggested that a better place to begin fighting segregation was to work to repeal miscegenation laws that prohibited inter-marriage or to work to remove segregation in public transportation.

Probably because of her own childhood experiences and because she did not really understand the lives of African-Americans in the 1950s, she argued that it was not important to integrate communities. What was important for human dignity was for political rights to be achieved on an equal basis for all. Arendt's article contributed to the heated debate on whether or not social change can be legislated. Many of her friends and associates thought that her analysis contributed to the wrong side of this debate, the side that maintained that legislation cannot contribute to positive social change. Moreover, Arendt had deep respect of the United States Constitution and argued for the importance of State's rights. This served to strengthen the judgment that Arendt's position was exceedingly conservative.

At the time, Arendt was not persuaded by any of her critics. However, in an interview given by Ralph Ellison to Robert Penn Warren in 1965, Ellison provided an explanation that finally convinced Arendt that her analysis had been limited, and so incorrect. Ellison explained that what Arendt did not understand was that in the United

States, every African-American needs to face terror and learn to control and restrain fear. Anyone who is unable to control the fears and tensions created by the racial situation will have a more difficult life. Parents in Little Rock were not asking their children to do anything unusual. They were simply helping their children face the realities of their lives.

While Arendt acknowledged Ellison's point, she remained concerned that education not be used to secure political ends. She believed that this could quickly lead to indoctrination and could destroy the hope and promise of new generations of young people. Instead, in "The Crisis in Education," printed in *Partisan Review*, she argued that education needed to provide children with an entry into the world of adults, the political world, while also protecting them. Education needs to introduce children to the world as adults create and value it, but it must also preserve their spontaneity so that they will be able to change that world, providing it with new beginnings.

The Eichmann Trial

In 1960, Adolf Eichmann was kidnapped by Israeli agents in Argentina and taken to Israel for trial. Eichmann had served in the Gestapo under Heinrich Himmler. He had primary responsibility for organizing the transportation that took Jews to internment camps and so to their deaths. Arendt offered to go to the trial as a reporter for the *New Yorker*. When she wrote Jaspers that she was going to the trial in this capacity, he urged her to reconsider writing,

> *You have taken on a great deal but have the equanimity to cancel those things that you cannot manage properly. The Eichmann trial will be no pleasure for you. I'm afraid it cannot go well. I fear your criticism and think that you will keep as much of it as possible to yourself.* (Letter 267)

Jaspers thought that Israel's integrity would be undermined in the trial no matter what happened. He recognized that the kidnapping was illegal and that there was much more than legal issues at stake. He also believed that Israel could not speak for Jewish people as a group. He thought that the case itself should be separated from a presentation of the facts about the holocaust. He thought that the case should be tried in another location, which should be selected by the United Nations.

Arendt took Jaspers' concerns seriously, and they influenced her approach to the trial, but she insisted that she had to go. She wrote to Jaspers,

> *I would never be able to forgive myself if I didn't go and look at this walking disaster face to face in all his bizarre vacuousness, without the mediation of the printed word. Don't forget how early I left Germany and how little of all this I really experienced directly.* (Letter 271)

Arendt arranged to attend the trial.

Arendt's account of the trial appeared in five articles in the *New Yorker*. Publication was delayed until 1963 because she was involved in an automobile accident. Later these articles were edited into the book, *Eichmann in Jerusalem* (See Chapter 4). Her work included a description of Eichmann that showed him to be a pathetic person rather than an inhuman monster. She labeled the phenomenon that she saw exemplified in Eichmann, the banality of evil.

Arendt's account of the Eichmann trial precipitated an immediate outrage. Jewish organizations accused her of being anti-Semitic and organized a campaign against her. Some of her best friends were so deeply disturbed by the work that their friendships with Arendt were fractured. Kurt Blumenfeld died while angry with her, and Hans Jonas went without speaking to her for over a year. They renewed their friendship on the grounds that the issue of Eichmann would never be discussed.

Readers of the book today may have difficulty understanding the controversy because they can appreciate the analysis that Arendt brought to the trial. However, at the time, Arendt's position was both challenging and threatening. In the aftermath of outcry about the book, Arendt herself began to focus on the type of thinking and judging that is needed to prevent the power of the banality of evil from prevailing. Some of her final works reflect this concern.

The Years on Riverside Drive

Arendt and Blücher moved one more time to a more spacious apartment on Riverside Drive. The apartment gave them a view of the Hudson River and provided a place for their many friends to come for conversation. Arendt continued to write and reflect on political issues. In 1963, she published *On Revolution*, which examined the French and the American Revolutions. Arendt believed that the American Revolution held more promise than the French because of the constitution writing that was part of the American Revolution.

She was excited by the student activity that arose in response to the war in Vietnam. She also approved of the student movements in 1968. However, when students took over offices at Columbia in 1968, she thought that they had gone too far and were posing a threat to academic freedom. She began to reflect on the use of violence in civil disobedience and wrote *On Violence*, which was published in 1970. She discouraged the use of violence because she believed that it introduced violence into the world.

While she was working on this book, her mentor and friend, Karl Jaspers, died. He was 86. At the service in his memory, Arendt said,

> *Every so often someone emerges among us who realizes human existence in an exemplary way and is the bodily incarnation of something that we would otherwise know only as a concept or ideal. In a singular way, Jaspers exemplified in himself, as it were, a fusion of freedom, reason, and communication. In his life he represented that fusion in exemplary form, so that...we from henceforth cannot think these three things...as separate but have to think them as a trinity.* (Arendt/Jaspers Correspondence 684-685)

In October of 1970, Heinrich Blücher died at home of a heart attack. Arendt had, just the day before, presented "Thinking and Moral Considerations" to the Society for Phenomenology and Existentialism, and had entertained J. Glen Gray in their home. Services were held for Blücher at the Riverside Chapel. W. H. Auden proposed that he and Arendt marry and take care of each other in their final years, but Arendt saw no merit in the proposal. She did, however, dedicate the published version of "Thinking and Moral Considerations" to Auden.

A Final Beginning

Arendt turned from her political emphasis in philosophy after Blücher's death and began writing more contemplative philosophy, *The Life of the Mind*. She gave the Gifford Lectures in 1973 and developed the first volume of the work, "Thinking." In 1974, she was prepared to give the second set of Gifford Lectures on "Willing" when she had a heart attack. She returned to New York where she died on December 4, 1975. The paper in her typewriter contained the title for the third volume, "Judging." Services were held for her at Riverside chapel and *Kaddish* was said.

Hannah Arendt is often judged to have been motivated by a love of the world. Clearly, her philosophical work demonstrates the promise and hope that she identifies as vital to human life. Even in the midst of thorough analysis of some of the most horrendous world events, she is able to resist the destructive power of the events by recognizing the possibility of new beginnings. Her writings manifest this hope.

2
Totalitarianism

Hannah Arendt and Heinrich Blücher recognized that they lived in a time in which an old order had died and something new had not yet emerged. They recognized that the twentieth century was a time of homelessness and of both hope and fear. While Arendt writes *The Origins of Totalitarianism*, the work represents their joint effort to comprehend their own experiences as well as the century in which they lived. Arendt explains the nature of this comprehension,

> *It means . . . examining and bearing consciously the burden which our century has placed on us – neither denying its existence nor submitting meekly to its weight. Comprehension, in short, means the unpremeditated, attentive facing up to, and resisting of, reality – whatever it may be.* (viii)

In *The Origins of Totalitarianism*, Arendt faces three destructive forces of the century in order to comprehend these forces and thereby point to ways of resisting them. She examines anti-Semitism, imperialism, and totalitarianism

In writing *The Origins of Totalitarianism*, Arendt also develops the philosophical framework that will provide her with the basis for the political and philosophical work that consumes the rest of her life. Her analysis is primarily historical; yet, it also begins to develop philosophical categories. She does not yet have all of these categories and concepts clearly articulated. They are present in a formative stage.

For example, she identifies the social as distinct from the private and the political and recognizes the growing influence of the social. She notes that with the loss of political groups there is also a loss of an understanding of a common humanity. She recognizes that a concept of abstract human equality does not provide for human unity and a common world.

Anti-Semitism

Arendt begins the three-part analysis of totalitarianism with a volume that focuses on anti-Semitism. As a Jew, she experienced the impact of anti-Semitism far more than Blücher, who was not Jewish. Yet, Arendt is concerned to comprehend anti-Semitism within the context of the European experience. She argues that anti-Semitism must be understood as an essential part of the totalitarianism that emerges in the twentieth century. She distinguishes between hatred of Jews and anti-Semitism. She argues that anti-Semitism emerges only when Jews and Gentiles are distinguished by racial, rather than religious, categories. She examines the elements of nineteenth-century history that show the rise of anti-Semitism, particularly as it contributes to the origins of totalitarianism. She maintains that there is no simple explanation of anti-Semitism. Political, economic, and social factors all contribute to the development of anti-Semitism.

Political and Economic Beginnings of Anti-Semitism

In her treatment of anti-Semitism, Arendt begins with an examination of the history of the relationship of the Jews to the state in order to identify the growth in hostility between Jews and other groups in the state. She believes that two often-voiced explanations of anti-Semitism are too simplistic. The explanation that Jews are arbitrarily selected scapegoats usually breaks down as soon as it is used. Further explanation as to why the Jews are selected seems necessary. The second explanation, that anti-Semitism as it emerges in the nineteenth-century is simply a further development in a long history of hatred of Jews, does not recognize the political nature of anti-Semitism. Arendt argues that anti-Semitism cannot be comprehended without understanding some of the complex political and economic events that give rise to "the moment when social discrimination changed into a political argument" (25).

Arendt traces the rise of anti-Semitism to the rise of the nation-state. As nationalism developed, Jews began to seek admission to non-Jewish society. She notes that in the seventeenth and eighteenth centuries certain wealthy Jews obtained positions in courts because they were able to finance affairs for the state. As nation-states developed after the French revolution, more wealth was needed to finance transactions. Certain families, such as the Rothchilds, emerged as the bankers of the Jewish communities' wealth and began to serve international business. Jews were granted political rights and so power in the financially developing nation-states. However, as imperialism grew, Gentile business people took over Jewish power and influence. Jewish influence declined. Jews became people who had "wealth without function" (4). Arendt notes that resentment emerges when there is wealth dissociated from power and so from state identity. Jews were viewed as no longer serving their states and so as a threat to those states.

Arendt reviews additional political events that also influenced the emergence of anti-Semitism. She argues that all of these events further moved Jews to want to integrate into society. They began to discover that the way into the mainstream of society was to be admitted as exceptions, under what she terms the "aura of fame" (52). Jewish intellectuals became critics and collectors. They organized what was famous. In doing this, they again crossed the boundaries of states, and so became "symbols of Society as such and the objects of hatred for all those whom society did not accept" (53).

Society and Jewish Identity: Pariah and Parvenu

Arendt notes that even where Jews gained political rights and equality, admission into society in general was not easily achieved. The class structure of European societies prevented Jews from entering society either as an independent class or with the capability for social mobility in the existing classes. Arendt writes,

> *Society, confronted with political, economic, and legal equality for Jews, made it quite clear that none of its classes was prepared to grant them social equality, and that only exceptions from the Jewish people would be received.* (56)

Arendt uses the terms she learned from Blumenfeld, 'pariah' and 'parvenu,' to help articulate a comprehension of the Jewish situation.

Jews could assimilate into society only if they were viewed as special. These are the 'parvenu.' They are not really qualified to be where they are in society, but they are admitted there because they are Jewish. They are expected to rise above other Jews and not behave as Jews, yet they are also admitted because they are exotic. It is their Jewishness that makes them exotic. Jews who did not, and could not, assimilate in this manner are 'pariah,' outcastes. They are separated from those Jews who do assimilate and from all non-Jewish people. Jews admitted to society were viewed as unique against this background of socially unacceptable Jews. Eventually in Prussia, the 'parvenu' Jews were protected, had civic rights, and were distinguished from foreign Jews. Two groups of Jews emerged, the assimilated and those who did not belong.

However, the social situation for assimilated Jews remained ambiguous. They were part of a society that discriminated against ordinary Jews; yet, that same society gave the exceptional Jews admission to circles because they were Jews. Arendt writes of this situation that it "actually amounted to a feeling of being different from other men in the street because they were Jews, and different from other Jews at home because they were not like 'ordinary Jews'" (65).

When the issues about Jewish identity within the state were primarily political, being Jewish could be considered a crime. However, Arendt recognizes that in the ambiguous social situation, being Jewish was transformed into a vice. To be Jewish is to be flawed. Arendt notes that Jews could escape from Judaism through conversion to Christianity. But Jewishness could not be escaped. In so far as Judaism was viewed as a crime, it could be punished through laws that restricted Jews. As a vice, it could only be eradicated. Arendt concludes,

> *The interpretation given by society to the fact of Jewish birth and the role played by Jews in the framework of social life are intimately connected with the catastrophic thoroughness with which antisemitic devices could be put to work. The Nazi brand of antisemitism had its roots in these social conditions....* (87)

Arendt maintains that anti-Semitism, which judged each individual Jew to be flawed, was already present in what is known as the Dreyfus affair.

21

The Dreyfus Affair

Arendt maintains that the Dreyfus affair provides a "foregleam of the twentieth century" (93). It shows how the political and social complexities of the nineteenth-century work together to foster anti-Semitism.

Alfred Dreyfus, a French Jewish officer, was convicted of espionage for Germany in 1894. The trial was followed by a series of attempts to show Dreyfus' innocence. Many were passionate in their effort to combat what they recognized to be an injustice. A series of trials resulted in changes in the original sentence. The Court of Appeals finally annulled Dreyfus' conviction in 1906 under the government of Prime Minister Clemenceau. Arendt maintains that this case shows the growing rise in anti-Semitism where hatred of Jews combines with mistrust of the state government. The government is perceived as under the controlling influence of Jews, especially the bankers. So, the Jews are understood as the source of corruption in the government.

Arendt traces the events of the period to show that those who supported Dreyfus firmly believed in the objective justice of the political system that made each person equal before the law. Their concern for Dreyfus stemmed from this commitment. However, other events, such as corruption associated with the building of the Panama Canal and the growing influence of the Jesuits in France served to challenge this comprehensive character of the law. Some issues were placed outside of the law where special interests prevailed. Arendt suggests that the final decision in the Dreyfus Affair was made in the social arena rather than in the appropriate legal arena. Thus, the Dreyfus Affair shows the growing influence of the social realm over the realm of the political. Later, in *The Human Condition*, Arendt develops this notion of the rise of the social in more detail. In *The Origins of Totalitarianism*, she simply notes that the Jewish question is one of the issues that is placed outside of the law.

Arendt's analysis uses the Dreyfus Affair to illustrate how anti-Semitism arises from the social ambiguities of the nineteenth century as well as from tensions between a politics of equality and a politics of special interest. Jews are accused of being the source of the corruption of democratic government and at the same time are excluded from the equal protection of the law. When she writes *The Human Condition*, she develops this analysis to show the impact of the social realm when it overpowers the political.

Imperialism

The second volume of Arendt's work on totalitarianism focuses on imperialism. Her approach continues to be historical, yet she also continues to develop the philosophical categories that are important for the rest of her thought. Moreover, she hopes that humans can learn from history even if they cannot know the future. She focuses on the period between 1884 and 1914, the period of imperialism.

Race-Thinking and Racism

Arendt maintains that nineteenth-century thought about race does not lead inevitably to racism, but does serve to promote racism. Moreover, race-thinking serves imperialism and so is connected to a power politics that diminishes human rights.

Arendt traces German race-thinking, showing how the work of Count Arthur de Gobineau, in 1853, serves to promote the idea of Aryans as an elite group who were in danger because of democracy. The Aryans are portrayed as a type of nobility or aristocracy. A similar approach is taken in England. The British identify themselves as a noble race because they ensure certain human liberties and pass these down through the inheritance of generations. Arendt maintains that in each case, race-thinking begins to deny the principle of human equality. For the Germans, the Aryan race becomes a noble race. The British see themselves as a nobility of people in the midst of other, lesser, nations.

Arendt suggests that this race-thinking became racism when the European countries entered Africa and needed an explanation for their experience. She writes,

> *Race was the emergency explanation of human beings whom no European or civilized man could understand and whose humanity so frightened and humiliated the immigrants that they no longer cared to belong to the same human species.* (185)

Racism emerges in the context of imperialism and becomes a political device to further imperialism. Racism serves to make distinctions among humans and so to undermine the liberal idea of human equality.

23

Bureaucracy and the "Pan" Movements

If race served to justify political domination of one people over another, bureaucracy served to carry out that domination. Arendt maintains that race, as a device of imperialism, worked best in South Africa. Bureaucracy worked best in India where the British assumed that they had a responsibility to protect the humanity of the Indian people. Bureaucracy serves to accumulate power in the hands of a few, and so to remove power from others. It works against a democracy that advocates human equality and instead destroys the idea of a common humanity.

Meanwhile, in Europe, many pan-national movements developed. These movements also worked against the idea of a common humanity. They advocated a tribal nationalism and maintained that each individual is connected with the divine only through membership in a specific people. They held that such peoples do not have a political identity, but rather a social identity. An idea of a political realm in which each individual has equal political rights is destroyed by the idea of distinct peoples who have their identity through common social practices that are racially identifiable. Racism and bureaucracy work together in imperialism to destroy the idea of a common humanity and so of common human rights.

Human Rights

Arendt argues that in the nineteenth century, human rights are lost because these rights are dissociated from political identity. Her experience of being a person without citizenship, and so without rights, leads her to maintain that there are no human rights for those who do not have political identity.

Humans are not equal because of their mere humanness. Indeed, Arendt maintains that when all that a person has is his or her humanness, it is difficult for others to treat that person as human. In contemporary times, those who live on the street serve as examples to support her analysis. Street people have nothing but their humanity. They have few, if any, possessions and nowhere to live. It would seem that this bare humanity would arouse the deep compassion of others. Instead, their mere humanity makes it difficult for others to see and to treat them as human. Only when advocacy groups argue for the rights of such people is their human equality acknowledged. Arendt writes, "We are not born equal; we become equal as members of a group on the strength of our decision to guarantee ourselves mutually equal rights" (301).

When people are excluded from equal rights, they are cast out of the common world. Arendt argues that this results in an internal danger for the very civilization that reduces these people to their mere humanity.

Totalitarianism

The third volume of *The Origins of Totalitarianism* addresses the issue of totalitarianism directly. It is rich in historical details. Arendt argues that totalitarianism is not simply a form of tyranny. She develops a powerful image for the distinction between tyranny and totalitarianism. Tyranny is a political form that is like a desert, presenting conditions that make human life difficult. Totalitarianism is a sand storm that covers all life, suffocating and eradicating the world. This volume was revised in the 1966 edition to show the connections between Nazi totalitarianism and Stalin's totalitarianism.

Arendt's examination of totalitarianism is one of the most extensive and influential works on the topic. It is particularly important for the description that Arendt develops of mass psychology and of totalitarianism as a movement.

Mass Psychology

Arendt maintains that totalitarianism was able to emerge because of the development of what she terms 'the masses.' She argues that the breakdown of class structures in the nineteenth century results in the emergence of the phenomenon of the masses. As class structure broke down in Europe, no structures emerged which could hold people together because of common interest. Arendt maintains that without common interest, people develop a mass psychology.

Arendt describes the masses as composed of isolated and lonely individuals. As class distinctions broke down, a type of atomistic individualism came to dominate human relations. People did not develop social links and did not recognize social obligations. These people were politically neutral because they did not have ties to members of a group. However, they still demonstrated a competitive spirit and so "acquired the appetite for political organization" (311). They could be organized, not because of commonly held needs or goals, but to serve the purposes of a minority.

Arendt claims that the invasion of parliamentary governments by totalitarian movements exemplifies this characteristic of the masses. Political parties and parliamentary majorities, vital to the constitutions of the countries, were identified by the totalitarian movements as unnecessary and, in fact, working against the real needs of the countries. Democratic freedoms, especially the concept of majority rule, were used to abolish freedom. Arendt says of totalitarianism,

> *The practical goal of the movement is to organize as many people as possible within its framework and to set and keep them in motion; a political goal that would constitute the end of the movement simply does not exist.* (326)

The masses, isolated individuals without common goals and social ties, serve the success of totalitarianism.

Characteristics of Totalitarianism

While totalitarianism uses terror, propaganda is a more important tool of totalitarianism. Arendt suggests that propaganda is particularly effective with the masses because they trust their imaginations more than their senses. Because they are isolated, they do not share in a common sense. That means that they do not use each other to check and confirm their experiences. Arendt maintains that people who are isolated in this manner are convinced by consistency rather than by facts. Propaganda is successful because its repetition is consistent over time (351).

Arendt claims that for totalitarianism, propaganda and organization are "two sides of the same coin." Propaganda provides the images of a fictitious world. Totalitarian organization takes the fiction and makes it function as reality. It develops organizational structures that lead the members of the society to "act and react according to the rules of a fictitious world" (364). These structures serve to protect and distance people from the authentic reality of the world, while at the same time allowing them to accept the fiction as reality.

Arendt identifies the structure of 'front organizations' as particularly unique and important to totalitarianism. The distinction between sympathizers and members of a totalitarian party illustrates the structure and importance of front organizations. The sympathizers are the front organization. Sympathizers protect the members of the party from the realities of the world. Members of the Nazi party were able to view themselves as connected with reality because the sympathizers served as their measure of what was normal. The Nazis did not recognize the fiction of their own position because the sympathizers, who were considered normal, believed the Nazi position to be plausible. In addition to protecting the members from the reality of the world, the sympathizers also serve as a front to the external world. The front organization serves to present the totalitarian movement to the outside world with a face that appears acceptable. It also presents the external world to the totalitarian movement in a way that convinces the movement that it is attuned to reality.

Arendt suggests that the organizational structure within totalitarianism makes use of this sort of 'front organization' at each level. "As party members are related to and separated from the fellow-travelers, so are the elite formations of the movement related to and separated from the ordinary members" (367). Totalitarianism develops its fiction by protecting each level in its organization from facing the truth of reality. Each level sees itself as correct because of the next lower level, which, in each case, reflects the fiction as truth and, at the same time, protects the higher level from penetrating to the truth.

In addition to developing this new organizational structure, totalitarian organization also makes use of secret societies where members must show that they are not part of the excluded group. In Nazi Germany, members were required to show that they were not Jewish. These secret societies included rituals that served to hold the members of the society together.

Totalitarian organization reconceives the meaning of power. Power is not based in material possessions. Power is a "force produced through organization" (418). Material concerns are secondary to organizational structures. Arendt notes that this is confirmed in Hitler's SS. Hitler was able to watch the destruction of Germany. Only when he realized that the organization of the SS troops could no longer be trusted did he recognize defeat.

All of the organizational structures of totalitarianism further the movement towards total domination. While the masses may enter totalitarianism out of their sense of isolation and loneliness, totalitarianism does not provide people with an understanding of their

27

uniqueness. Rather, it serves to reduce all humans to the identity of one individual. The Füher is the exemplar of human reality. Those who do not meet this model, those who show uniqueness and spontaneity, are exterminated.

Arendt maintains that totalitarian organization does reflect the realities of human experience in that it emphasizes "the experience of modern masses of their superfluity on an overcrowded earth" (457). Arendt suggests that this organizational structure of totalitarianism may have disclosed the meaning of radical evil. Later, when she attends the Eichmann trial, she will modify this position, suggesting that totalitarianism actually discloses the banality of evil.

Comprehending and Resisting the Sand Storm

At the end of *The Origins of Totalitarianism*, Arendt asks the question with which she began her inquiry. What experience of human living together makes possible the emergence of totalitarianism? Several hundred pages of detailed historical analysis developed in the context of emerging philosophical concepts lead her to comprehend the phenomenon of totalitarianism in a seemingly simple manner. What humans must face is that they have become isolated and lonely.

Isolation is the human situation in relation to the political sphere. Instead of having common needs and goals, humans experience themselves as separated. This diminishes their political power because they no longer act together for a common goal. If people were merely isolated, they might be able to avoid the disaster of totalitarianism. However, they are also lonely. Loneliness is the experience "of not belonging to the world at all" (475).

Totalitarianism is the sand storm that is able to cover the world and so confirm that humans no longer belong to a world. Once this is comprehended, the question remains for Arendt as to whether or not totalitarianism can be resisted. Her answer is hopeful, but incomplete. She suggests that the hope is for a new beginning before totalitarianism can reach its potential to end the world. Her hope is in the guarantee of the birth of each new person.

This is a delicate hope that Arendt maintains throughout her life. As she moves on to write *The Human Condition*, she retains this hope and further develops many of the concepts and categories that are important to her analysis of *The Origins of Totalitarianism*.

The historical and political analysis that she does in this early work sets the direction for all of the rest of her thought. She will further articulate the distinctions among the private, social, and public. She will define and distinguish labor, work, and action. She will examine the role of thought for the active life, and she will continually hope for the possibility of new beginnings. Yet, while her work is hopeful, it is also always aware that the sand storm of totalitarianism is a constant threat. The possibility of totalitarian domination did not end with the death of Stalin. It is a reality that has emerged in history and remains a threat for the human world.

3

The Human Condition

The Human Condition is Hannah Arendt's major philosophical work. The project that she proposes for this book is "to think what we are doing" (5). She begins, as she did with *The Origins of Totalitarianism*, in the context of her experience and the experience of the times in which she lived. Arendt wrote this book at the time when humans were beginning flights into space and as technology was becoming increasingly important. She recognizes that these new experiences also give rise to fears and contribute to the isolation and loneliness that she has identified as part of the human experience in the twentieth century. In *The Human Condition*, she proposes an analysis that will help humanity face and resist the movement towards alienation.

Arendt insists in this work, as she does in all of her thought, on the importance of analysis of the historical situation. She is concerned to show how modern alienation has emerged out of historical conditions. She traces the human flight from the earth to the universe and from the world to the self, showing the development of contemporary alienation. However, the work is more than an analysis of history. It is also an attempt to identify what is so fundamental to the human condition that it must be preserved if we are to remain human.

In carrying out her analysis, Arendt focuses on what she terms the *vita activa*, the active life. This means that she does not examine the *vita contemplativa*, the contemplative life. She recognizes that thinking is in many ways the most human activity, but she proposes to restrict her analysis to "those activities that traditionally, as well as according to current opinion, are within the range of every human being" (5). Arendt's later writings treat the importance of thought for preserving a human world. However, in *The Human Condition*, she focuses on what she takes to be the three fundamental human activities: labor, work, and action.

Public, Private, and Social

Before addressing each type of human activity, Arendt maintains that it is important to situate the activities. She makes use of and further develops the distinctions that she used in *The Origins of Totalitarianism*. She identifies the private, the public, and the social as the three realms in which human action takes place. In explaining these three realms, she offers a description of what emerged historically. However, she also develops these three realms in order to provide criteria for helping us determine how to understand the place of the various forms of human action.

The Private Realm and the Public Realm

In explaining the distinction between the private and the public, Arendt turns to Greek beginnings. The influence of Heidegger's phenomenology is clear in this move. This phenomenological approach maintains that we must retrieve the history of the concepts with which we function, in order to understand these concepts. This retrieval enables us to discover possibilities for opening our own futures. Since Western civilization has its origins in ancient Greek life and thought, it is important to reflect on those origins. It is worth noting that Arendt does not advocate returning to the distinctions as they were lived in ancient Greek society. She recognizes that this Greek democracy included the acceptance of slavery and excluded many people from the public realm, which is the realm of freedom. Despite these limitations, she maintains that important insights contained in Greek thought may help us think about what we are doing today. She identifies the concepts of the private and the public as of particular importance.

Arendt notes that ancient Greek society drew a clear distinction

31

between the private realm and the public realm. She maintains that this distinction identifies the private realm as pre-political. It is the arena of natural association and centers on the family and the home. The political realm is the realm of action and speech, the realm of freedom. While both of these spheres, as understood by the ancient Greeks, are gone from contemporary society, the activities that belonged to each of these realms remain part of human activity. Arendt believes that it is important to understand the activities that were delegated to each realm in order to recognize how these activities are transformed as the distinction between the two spheres breaks down.

According to Arendt, in ancient Greece, the private realm was the realm ruled by necessity, addressing human wants and needs. The family and home gave structure to this realm. In this structure, rule was absolute. Men's individual wants and needs were met, and women served to meet the wants and needs of the species. There was strict inequality. Force and violence were justified in the private realm because they were needed in order to conquer necessity. Arendt notes that economics belonged in this sphere in ancient Greece and so was not political. Property was part of the structure of the household. Indeed, without the base of property, a man could not enter the public sphere. The private sphere enabled a man to liberate himself from necessity and so enter a second life in the public sphere.

Yet, the private realm also provided shelter from the public sphere for those activities that needed to remain hidden. Arendt makes use of goodness to illustrate that not everything that needs to remain hidden, that needs to be sheltered from the public, is destructive or corrupt. She writes, "Goodness can exist only when it is not perceived, not even by its author; whoever sees himself performing a good work is no longer good, but at best a useful member of society or a dutiful member of a church"(74). Arendt finds a similarity between goodness and wisdom in this hiddenness. As Socrates understood, the wisest person is the one who recognizes that no one can be wise. Arendt believes that goodness is an even more extreme example of the need for hiddenness. She says, "Good works, because they must be forgotten instantly, can never become part of the world; they come and go, leaving no trace. They are truly not of this world" (76). While the private sphere as delineated in ancient Greece may seem very oppressive to contemporary people, Arendt's point in using the illustration of goodness is to emphasize that there are activities that need to remain hidden because of the very nature of the activity. Yet, the private sphere in ancient Greece primarily denoted a realm of privation, a realm in which many were not free and so did not actualize the highest of human capacities.

The public realm in ancient Greece was the realm of action and speech, the realm of the political. It was the realm of freedom for the building of a common human world, and so was understood to involve the most truly human part of life. In the public realm, decisions were made through persuasion. Violence, while acceptable in the private sphere, was not a viable means of action in the public realm. The public was the realm in which individuals were equal before each other and where they could excel and distinguish themselves, showing their individual differences.

Such a strong distinction between private and public clearly had drawbacks. For example, women and slaves were kept from participating in the fully human activities that were reserved for the public sphere. Yet, Arendt identifies the most positive aspect of the clear distinction as the separation of activities that address the necessities of human life and those that express human freedom. She writes,

> *Being seen and being heard by others derive their significance from the fact that everybody sees and hears from a different position. This is the meaning of public life, compared to which even the richest and most satisfying family life can offer only the prolongation or multiplication of one's own position with its attending aspects and perspectives.* (57)

Holding the public apart from the private enables at least some people to recognize that human diversity is fundamental to the fullness of human life. Unique individuals work together in the public realm to create a human world, a world that transcends the force of necessity.

Arendt maintains that beginning with the dominance of Roman civilization and on through the medieval period, the clear distinction between the private and the public began to disappear. In addition, a new realm, the social, began to emerge.

The Social Realm

Arendt describes the social realm as formed when housekeeping emerges into the light of the public sphere. She maintains that as Roman and then medieval Christian civilization developed, there was a change in the way in which the necessities of life were handled.

Instead of being the concern of individual households, these activities moved outside of the household structure. As this happened, the lines between the private and the political began to blur and the meanings of the two spheres began to alter.

The public sphere, as understood in ancient Greece, was greatly diminished. The rise of the social in the context of housekeeping activities means that members of a given society are expected to act "as though they were members of one enormous family which has only one opinion and one interest" (39). Members of a society are expected to obey rules and conform to the norms of society rather than speak and act as individuals. This means that the activities that express human distinctiveness and distinction, associated with the Greek understanding of the public realm, are diminished in value and even moved into the private realm. Equality in its modern social form has its basis in social conformity rather than in the political understanding of unique speaking and acting. Arendt writes, "behavior has replaced action as the foremost mode of human relationship" (41). When the social emerges as the primary realm of human interaction, then rules of conformity are more important than individual identity and distinctness.

While Arendt recognizes the limitations of the Greek form of democracy, she does not view the development of the social realm as an advance. The problem with Greek democracy was that it depended on household structures that served to exclude many people from the public realm of freedom. Arendt does not believe that moving the activities of housekeeping into the social arena results in moving more people into freedom. Rather, it serves to diminish human freedom.

Arendt believes that the contemporary reliance on statistics exemplifies this point. Statistics are not valid for small numbers and for short periods of time. When we understand ourselves through statistics we find meaning in patterns of behavior for large groups over extended time, not in individual events. Yet, Arendt maintains that "the meaningfulness of everyday relationships is disclosed not in everyday life but in rare deeds, just as the significance of a historical period shows itself only in the few events that illuminate it" (42). If we lose sight of the importance of those unique events that illuminate human life, we risk losing the most fully human aspects of our world.

Political structures that develop in the context of the domination of the social replace personal rule with bureaucracy. Arendt calls this the rule of nobody. She sees government as giving way to administration. She notes that Karl Marx was correct in his analysis that the state would wither away. But she believes that he was wrong in thinking that this would result in an enhancement of the realm of freedom.

Instead, the freedom to speak and act openly is diminished. The social sphere has a tendency to grow and "devour the older realms of the political and private" (45).

The private sphere no longer serves to contain the activities of meeting the necessities of life. It also no longer serves to shelter people from the political. The private sphere is defined in relationship to the social rather than the political and shelters the intimate from the social. Moreover, the activities of speaking and acting as individuals, the activities of the old political realm, are moved into this new private realm. Individual difference is viewed as an intimate matter, to be hidden from public view. The private does continue to serve the function of concealing. But in relation to modern society, this hiding now contributes to the loneliness of twentieth-century people. The private is an inner space, and so expressing one's individuality becomes more and more an internal activity.

The role of private property is also changed as the social grows and displaces the former private realm. Arendt maintains that in ancient Greece, "property meant no more or less than to have one's location in a particular part of the world and therefore to belong to the body politic" (61). To have a private space of one's own was essential for entering the public sphere. Private property, in this sense, was sacred. It was the space in which birth and death took place. As the social has grown, private property has been displaced by the accumulation of wealth. Private property is understood as privately owned wealth, not as the place from which to enter and retreat from public life. Neither individual nor social appropriations of wealth continue the role of private property in guaranteeing entry into a realm of freedom. This change in the understanding of property illustrates the absorption of the private into the social and also shows the potential political risks of this absorption.

In the contemporary world, Arendt believes that we live primarily in the social realm. While this realm diminishes human freedom, Arendt does not believe that we are powerless. We can act in ways to increase and restore human freedom. We can resist the social. Knowledge of the original role of the private and the public realms may help us to understand our own actions and their implications for building a human world. The distinctions, especially as originally draw between the public and the private, may help us to have a clearer understanding of the importance and place of the three types of human activities: labor, work, and action.

Labor, Work, and Action

Arendt's description and analysis of the realms or spaces in which human activity takes place correspond, in part, to the three types of activity that she identifies as fundamental to the human condition. Labor belongs primarily with the private realm. Work relates to the social realm although it also tends to bridge the private and the public realms. Action is the activity of the public and political realm. When trying to understand Arendt's analysis of these three activities, it is important to note that her use of the words "activities" and "action" can be confusing. She understands labor, work, and action as three activities of human life. Arendt believes that understanding each of these will help us to situate each activity in its most appropriate place in human life and also help us resist the tendency of the social to overtake the political and so reduce human freedom.

Labor and Consumerism

Humans are *homo laborans*, laboring beings. The human activity of labor focuses on meeting the necessities of life. Labor is primarily concerned with supporting life. This means that labor is devoted to meeting the subsistence and reproductive needs of human life. Labor involves human bodies. Labor is primarily a bodily activity and is focused on meeting the needs of the body. Moreover, labor mixes with things and so holds the body in close relation to the object that meets its needs. Arendt maintains that labor is a pre-human activity. It is shared with other species of animals. All animals labor to meet the basic necessities of life. Because of this, labor is most closely identified with the private realm. It forms the basis for a fully human life. However, in order for this fuller human life to be realized, people must move beyond the activity of labor.

Labor by itself moves in a circle. Arendt says that labor involves "the daily fight in which the human body is engaged to keep the world clean and prevent its decay" (101). Contemporary housework still exemplifies this circularity. The activities involved in maintaining a household are repetitive. As soon as laundry is finished, it needs to be done again. If Arendt is correct, housework cannot move a person to freedom. Rather, it confines a person who performs this activity to a pre-human life.

36

Arendt's description of labor also serves as a critique of Marx's analysis of labor. In opposition to Marx, Arendt maintains that labor does not define what it is to be human. Rather, labor is the activity in which humans engage that identifies them most closely with the rest of the animal kingdom. According to Arendt, Marx is correct in suggesting that production and consumption define labor. However, when humans are primarily concerned with the activity of labor, the result is a consumer society. In such a society, the focus on consumption directs people away from the more human concern of speaking and acting in ways that are able to create a human world that facilitates real freedom. Yet, labor gives rise to the human desire for a stable world, one that does not have to be constantly remade. The activity of labor points to the possibility of the activity of work.

Work and the Exchange Market

Humans are also *homo faber*, beings who make tools and objects for use. Arendt distinguishes labor from work in a manner that she admits is unusual (79). Yet, she argues that most languages clearly make this distinction. "Labor" and "work" are used in very different ways and, normally, cannot be substituted for each other. She particularly notes that,

> the word *"labor,"* understood as a noun, never designates the finished product, the result of laboring, but remains a verbal noun to be classed with the gerund, whereas the product itself is invariably derived from the word for work (80)

While labor deals with meeting the necessities of life, work is a human activity that has an instrumental character. While labor is a bodily activity, work has to do with human hands. The human activity of work constructs things that endure. This serves to stabilize human life. Arendt says that work promotes stability because, "Men, their ever-changing nature notwithstanding, can retrieve their sameness, that is their identity, by being related to the same chair and the same table" (137). The chair built by a grandparent conveys stability when it is used by a child of a further generation. The results of work are not consumed in the same manner as are the results of labor. Rather, work structures the world in a way that sustains it. While work involves the destruction of the natural, it also provides the transition from the natural to the most fully human types of activities.

If labor is related most closely to the private realm and so to the meeting of necessities, work is related most closely to the social. Work provides those objects that serve to sustain and structure a society. Work contributes to the structuring of a world that is more permanent than the ever-repeating cycle of labor. However, Arendt's analysis emphasizes the instrumental character of work and so the limitations of the sort of world that work produces. She says, "during the work process, everything is judged in terms of suitability and usefulness for the desired end, and for nothing else" (153). Because work focuses on the relationship of means to ends, everything becomes part of an ongoing chain of means and ends. What is identified as an end, quickly becomes a means to some further end. Everything is then judged in terms of its usefulness for some further end. Arendt notes that understanding humans as beings whose primary or defining activity is work leads to the understanding, most fully developed by the eighteenth-century philosopher Immanuel Kant, that humans are the only real end. Everything else has its value as a means for humans.

If an emphasis on human labor results in a consumer society, an emphasis on human work leads to the development of an exchange market. In this market, things have value only in relationship to other things and to human usefulness. Arendt maintains that an emphasis on the activity of work results in a world where utility is mistaken for meaning. Humans focus on what she calls "in order to" and forget "for the sake of." While the world created through work has a stability that labor cannot create, it is still a world that isolates people from each other and that is experienced as meaningless. Arendt's analysis clearly connects the problems of the social realm with a kind of human self-understanding that emphasizes the activity of work, of fabrication.

Yet, Arendt identifies a hopeful aspect of work in her analysis of the work of art. Because works of art are works that lack utility, they are able to reveal the world that humans have constructed in a unique way. Arendt writes,

It is as though worldly stability had become transparent in the permanence of art, so that a premonition of immortality, not the immortality of the soul or of life but of something immortal achieved by mortal hands, has become tangibly present, to shine and to be seen, to sound and to be heard, to speak and to be read. (168)

The work of art, while a human fabrication, also reveals the human "capacity for thought" and so points to the importance of constructing a world that is a place for human action.

Action and the Sphere of Appearance

Arendt maintains that the most fully human life is the *vita activa*, the active life. The activity of action presupposes human plurality. Unlike labor, which is a pre-human activity, and work, which keeps individuals isolated, action requires the company of other humans. Each person who forms part of the web of human plurality is distinct and unique, and all are equals.

Action, according to Arendt, is disclosive and establishes relationships. The primary form of disclosive activity is speech. Humans speak to disclose who they are. Arendt notes that this activity is not the activity of isolated individuals, but takes place among people. People disclose each other in conversations and stories in the public arena. Moreover, action "has an inherent tendency to force open all limitations and cut across all boundaries" (190). Action enables new beginnings to take place. Action enables people to organize themselves and so to constitute a common world.

Arendt calls this common world the "space of appearance" (199). This is the space where action and speech can appear in public. When people come together in this space, they create power and so also create political communities. Arendt writes,

> *Power is actualized only where word and deed have not parted company, where words are not empty and deeds not brutal, where words are not used to veil intentions but to disclose realities, and deeds are not used to violate and destroy but to establish relations and create new realities.* (200)

As long as people act and speak to disclose themselves, this space of appearance remains vital and so makes possible a vital political life. This means that the public sphere, while the appropriate realm for human action, is also constituted by human action. Therefore, human activity can also destroy the power that is possible in this space of appearance, the power that enables humans to appear in their full plurality.

When humans understand themselves as *homo faber* or as *homo laborans*, and see these activities as the greatest human achievements,

39

then the space of appearance atrophies. It can no longer grow to disclose human newness and uniqueness. Arendt illustrates this possible dangerous consequence for the sphere of appearance by reviewing what she has already noted about work and labor.

In work, people make things. They are fabricators. While the actual work of production is done in isolation, indirectly people are drawn into connection with each other in the exchange of products. Arendt acknowledges that this exchange does take place in the realm of action and so helps to form the sphere of appearance. However, she also maintains that "the people who meet on the exchange market are primarily not persons but producers of products, and what they show there is never themselves, ... but their products" (209). If humans understand themselves primarily as *homo faber*, then they fail to recognize that individuals transcend what they make. Who a person is, is more than what that person does or makes. For this aspect of human life to appear, a political realm is needed.

According to Arendt, understanding the human condition as defined by work results in an unpolitical life. However, understanding the human condition as primarily defined by labor results in antipolitical life. Arendt takes Marx's analysis of the alienation of labor seriously. While laborers live in the presence of others, she maintains that they are lonely, excluded from a life of plurality. She says that labor results in each person losing his or her "awareness of individuality and identity" (213). She illustrates this claim with the example of the importance of rhythm for people who labor together. Groups may sing in order to work together as one. But Arendt says, "This unitedness of many into one is basically antipolitical; it is the very opposite of the togetherness prevailing in political or commercial communities" (214). There is no possibility of disclosing individuality and distinctness in laboring activities. Understanding ourselves merely as laborers does not provide for the possibility of opening a sphere of appearance for political life.

The dangers posed to the sphere of appearance by emphasizing the activities of labor and work, and so minimizing action, show the fragility of the political sphere. Both the unpredictability and irreversibility of action increase the fragility of the sphere of appearance. Actions, because they begin new and spontaneous processes, are uncertain and uncontrollable. Yet, Arendt also finds hope in the possibilities of human action for maintaining a vital sphere of appearance. She identifies forgiveness and promise as powers that can help remedy the risks of action.

Arendt identifies forgiveness and promise as actions that must take place in the public realm and which also serve to nurture that realm. She says that both actions,

> *depend on plurality, on the presence and acting of others, for no one can forgive himself and no one can feel bound by a promise made only to himself; forgiving and promising enacted in solitude or isolation remain without reality and can signify no more than a role played before one's self.* (237)

Forgiveness enables us to redeem each other from the irreversibility of action. Promise enables us to counteract the unpredictability of action and so address the uncertainty of the future.

Arendt's emphasis on the importance of forgiveness and promise is based in her recognition that these actions always emphasize the 'who' of unique individuals. When we forgive and promise we help construct a sphere of appearance in which plurality can be recognized and affirmed. Arendt's hope for the human condition is based on the possibilities contained in forgiveness and promise. Both of these point her towards the insight of the importance of what she calls natality. While natality is connected to the fact that each person is born, it also shows us that we are born "in order to begin, " not in order to die. Our capacity to act is based in our natality. She maintains that the most succinct expression of hope for the world is found in the Gospel tiding, "A child has been born unto us" (247).

Thinking What We Are Doing

Arendt's analysis of the private, political, and social realms and of the activities of labor, work, and action are all preliminary to her examination of the modern age and the modern world. She distinguishes between the two, identifying the modern age as the period from the seventeenth to the twentieth century and the modern world as the political world that begins with the explosion of the first atomic bomb. In order to think what we are doing, and so prevent alienation and the social from engulfing and atrophying the sphere of appearance, Arendt believes that we must examine the modern age to better understand what spaces humans have constructed for disclosing themselves. This examination will place us in a position to ask what actions are most needed in the modern world if we are to construct and preserve a world where we can appear, that is, where we can disclose

41

each other in our human plurality.

The Modern Age

Arendt identifies three events that give beginning shape to the modern age: the exploration of America, the Reformation and its impact on wealth, and the invention of the telescope and the new science that results from this invention. These events all set a direction for what she calls world alienation. The event of scientific development is most helpful for understanding her analysis. Science illustrates how in the modern age people have moved away from a commonly shared and constituted world in two directions, outward into space and inward into isolated selves.

With the development of the telescope, humans became able to view the earth from space. Arendt uses the image of the Archimedean point to explain the movement that takes place. This is the point from which Archimedes claimed that he could move the earth. Arendt explains that in the modern age, this point is in the universe and outside the earth. We understand the earth and nature, not from a point situated within nature, but from an astrophysical point in space. While Arendt did not have the visual image of the earth as seen from space to illustrate her point, we now have such photographs. We can sit in our homes on the earth and view the earth from space. Because of this, we can treat the earth as though we were outside of it, even while we live on it. Arendt points out that this transcendence of the earth is also an alienation from the world of common experience. She explains that humans have won a freedom from "earth-bound experience" but at the same time have placed nature under conditions of the mind (265).

The telescope calls into question the reliability of the senses and so calls into question human agreement on the nature of a common world. More significantly, this event calls into question the goodness of God and pushes people to move into their isolated selves for any sense of certainty. For example, people continue to experience the sun rising and setting, and yet know that this is an illusion. This experience leads them to recognize that they can no longer be certain of their common world. Arendt says that humans can no longer be sure that they inhabit and share a common world; all they can be certain of is that they have the structure of their minds in common. She explains that the highest ideal for the modern age is

> *not the knowledge of ideal forms given outside the mind but of*
> *forms produced by a mind which in this particular instance does*
> *not even need the stimulation – or, rather, the irritation – of the*
> *senses by objects other than itself.* (283)

The common world is no longer constituted by individuals whose private sensations must fit together. Rather, what people have in common is a faculty of reasoning. However, each person's mind plays with only itself and so is cut off from, alienated from, a common world. The modern age has not created a sphere of appearance where humans can speak openly with each other. Rather, it has removed us from the earth and pushed us into isolation and loneliness.

The Modern World and the Importance of Thought

The modern world emerged out of the modern age with the explosion of the atomic bomb. What humans cannot now deny is that we can know only what we make ourselves. There is not an external or transcendent world of eternal truth that gives stability to the mortal world. Only humans can construct and know a common world. Arendt notes that this insight can lead us to "redoubled activity or to despair" (293). The way of redoubled activity is preferable and will involve thought as well as action.

Arendt excludes considerations of the *vita contemplativa* from *The Human Condition*. Yet, her concluding sentence for the book quotes Cato and carries the implication that thinking is, perhaps, the most important of human activities. In a discussion about this book, in Toronto in 1972, Arendt said that the main flaw with *the Human Condition* was that "I still look at what is called in the traditions the *vita activa* from the viewpoint of the *vita contemplativa*, without ever saying anything real about the *vita contemplativa" (Hill 305)*. The question that remains for Arendt, and for the modern world, is "What is thinking good for?" She recognizes that thinking is not the same as acting and that thinkers are dishonest if they maintain that thinking is acting. Yet, thinking can influence action and also be vital for human life. The importance of thinking for the modern world occupies Arendt for the rest of her life.

4

Eichmann

Arendt brings the thinking that she has done in both *The Origins of Totalitarianism* and *The Human Condition* to her analysis of the trial of Adolf Eichmann. She is convinced that thought must begin with experience. In her analysis of the trial she calls on her experiences of the trial, on information related to the trial, and on information about the experiences of Jews during the war years. She also brings to her analysis the presupposition that individual action is of fundamental political importance. Arendt does not ever develop a political theory that advocates specific structures or changes in structures. Her main concern as a political thinker is to identify the kinds of actions that create and hold open the sphere of appearance, the political sphere. At the same time, she identifies those ways of life that destroy this political sphere. While her analysis of Eichmann is about evil, it is primarily about the connection between thinking and action and about the importance of thinking for the political.

In discussion about her analysis of the trial with Christian Bay, Professor of Political Economy at the University of Toronto, in 1972, Hannah Arendt argues for the political importance of thinking. She disputes the contention that political theorists must seek to indoctrinate others. She speaks out of her experience as a teacher, emphasizing the importance of arousing thinking in students rather than trying to control the consequences of thinking. This is of fundamental importance because, *when the chips are down, the question is how they will act. And then this notion that I examine my assumptions, ... that I think "critically," and that I don't let myself get away with repeating the clichés of the public mood [comes into play]. And I would say that any society that has lost respect for this, is not in very good shape.* (Hill 309).

Arendt's emphasis on the importance of critical thinking and her rejection of indoctrination motivate her analysis of the Eichmann trial.

As with most of Arendt's writings, *Eichmann in Jerusalem* contains many pithy insights and takes many directions. In writing, Arendt tends to develop threads of thought that she comes back to many times. At the same time, her overall structure sometimes gets lost as the threads develop. This makes her work complex and also makes many diverse, and sometimes conflicting, interpretations more possible. More than any of her other work, *Eichmann in Jerusalem* elicited strong and conflicting responses. In order to understand Arendt's analysis it is most helpful to remember the importance of the connection between thinking and acting for Arendt's political thought. She makes use of this connection as she tries to understand Eichmann, the trial itself, and the actions of many people who lived through the times of the holocaust.

Eichmann

Adolf Eichmann was born in 1906 in Solingen, Germany. He moved to Linz, Austria when he was twenty-three. In 1932, he joined the Nazi Party and then Heinrich Himmler's SS. He worked in Dachau and then Berlin, advancing in the SS hierarchy. He was sent to Vienna in 1938 to rid the city of Jews and then to Prague for the same reason. After the Wannsee conference in 1942 where arrangements were made for the "final solution," Eichmann was appointed to coordinate the logistics for the transportation of Jews to the death camps. Eichmann escaped from U. S. troops in 1946 and eventually settled in Argentina. On May 11, 1960, Israeli secret service agents arrested him and smuggled him out of Argentina. He was tried in Israel between April 11 and December 15, 1961. He was sentenced to hang and was executed.

In *Eichmann in Jerusalem*, Arendt says of Eichmann, "The longer one listened to him, the more obvious it became that his inability to speak was closely connected with an inability to *think*, namely, to think from the standpoint of somebody else" (49). This insight, more than any other, leads her to subtitle the book, *A Report on the Banality of Evil*. In *The Human Condition*, when reflecting on evil, she notes that we call some evil radical because we can neither punish nor forgive it. In Eichmann, she sees a man who does not embody radical evil. His motives are not evil, even though what he does contributes to evil. He is unthinking, and so he contributes to those things which make humans superfluous. While Arendt is accused of minimizing the crimes of Eichmann, her analysis does not support the conclusion that Eichmann is not guilty of, or responsible for, crimes. Rather, she presents Eichmann as a dilemma that needs to be addressed and understood.

The dilemma that Eichmann represents is present because Eichmann is "normal." Indeed, Arendt notes that a number of psychiatrists certified him as "normal" and the prison minister found him to have positive ideas. Arendt concludes that what Eichmann reveals is that a perfectly normal person can be "incapable of telling right from wrong" (26). In the context of the Third Reich, Eichmann was a law-abiding citizen who saw no reason to judge his own actions as criminal. Arendt maintains that those involved in the case missed its "greatest moral and legal challenge" by not addressing this dilemma. Her analysis seeks to understand how Eichmann could be normal. She uses his memoirs as well as trial testimony to develop her understanding. She demonstrates that Eichmann is normal, because being normal requires behavior, not thought.

Arendt documents in great detail the fact that Eichmann had a life-long pattern of behaving without thinking. For example, she notes that he joined the Nazi Party without information. He reports that Ernst Kaltenbrunner suggested it to him and he thought "Why not?" (33). He also claims to have joined the SS by mistake, thinking that it was an entirely different security service.

Arendt especially emphasizes the manner in which Eichmann's use of language illustrates his total lack of thought. She notes that he spoke in and depended on clichés, officialese, and language rules. When asked to explain his reasons for joining the Party, he answers in clichés about "the Treaty of Versailles and unemployment" (33). Later, when asked to admit his crimes, he explains that "he would like to find peace with [his] former enemies." Arendt notes that when Eichmann uses these clichés, he has a sense of elation. She writes,

> *Eichmann's mind was filled to the brim with such sentences.*
> *His memory proved to be quite unreliable about what had actually*

happened; . . . But the point of the matter is that he had not forgotten a single one of the sentences of his that at one time or another had served to give him a "sense of elation." (53)

She found him incapable of speaking in anything but clichés (48). She notes that even at his death he used clichés, elated to the point that he forgot that it "was his own funeral" (252).

Eichmann also followed language rules, using code words such as "final solution" and "special treatment" instead of "killing." As part of the Security Service, Eichmann was a "bearer of secrets" and so was given "language rules" as part of his orders. For example, the International Red Cross wanted to visit the Bergen-Belsen concentration camp in addition to Theresienstadt, which was maintained as the showable concentration camp. Eichmann was given "language rules" and ordered to explain that there was an outbreak of typhus at Bergen-Belsen. Language rules made it possible for people to lie without thinking that they were doing anything wrong. Arendt notes that "Eichmann's great susceptibility to catch words and stock phrases, combined with his incapacity for ordinary speech, made him, of course, an ideal subject for 'language rules'" (86).

Arendt's presentation of Eichmann as unthinking also emphasizes that Eichmann believed that he followed his conscience and did his duty. While he may have had some doubts about the Final Solution, his conscience was quickly soothed. He saw that no one else protested or refused to cooperate. Arendt suggests that conscience got lost in Germany. Conscience did not develop in a climate of thought, but rather in the context of mass society. Those who raised objections based on conscience were usually concerned that the war was not winnable and so harmed German society. They were not troubled by the extermination of Jews. Eichmann simply exemplified the general state of human conscience. He understood himself as a person who did his duty; that is, he obeyed the law. He did what the Führer would approve. He was a person of conscience because he did his duty even when it was against his inclination. In this behavior, he was a normal German. Arendt notes that the law was reversed in Hitler's Germany, such that the voice of conscience came to tell people, "Thou shalt kill." She writes, "Evil in the Third Reich had lost the quality by which most people recognize it – the quality of temptation" (150). Indeed, if there was temptation, it was the temptation not to kill. What in most cultures is considered good, became temptation in Germany. One was tempted not to betray one's neighbor.

Arendt views Eichmann as a lesson in the banality of evil because he shows so clearly what can happen when a person and a culture speak and behave without thinking. While many people object to Arendt's analysis because they think it excuses Eichmann, her analysis of Eichmann discloses the importance of thinking for preserving human life. She says of Eichmann, "It was sheer thoughtlessness – something by no means identical with stupidity – that predisposed him to become one of the greatest criminals of that period" (287-88).

The Trial

Arendt's concern to understand the Eichmann trial critically also leads her to reflect on the extent to which the trial represents justice. She questions and rejects Prime Minister David Ben-Gurion's goal for the trial. She admires the judges who hear the case and oversee the trial, yet she believes that they do not face all of the important legal and moral issues.

David Ben-Gurion was the Prime Minister of Israel who ordered Eichmann kidnapped from Argentina. Ben-Gurion wanted the trial of Eichmann to be in Israel. Arendt believed that he desired this, not because he thought that this was the place that justice could best be served, but because he thought that the youth of Israel needed to know what had happened in the holocaust. He wanted to try the German people for anti-Semitism and for the suffering of the Jews. He especially wanted Israeli youth to believe in the necessity and importance of Zionism as the movement that had enabled Jews to survive through the years of the holocaust. The trial, in his mind, had little to do with justice, and everything to do with indoctrination. Eichmann provided that opportunity. Gideon Hausner, the Attorney General, served as the spokesperson for this position during the trial and was praised for his success at the end of the trial.

Arendt judges the Israeli position to be both illegal and unthinking. Israel had no right to kidnap Eichmann. In addition, Israel ignored justice in trying Eichmann for crimes against the Jews, rather than for the crimes that he as an individual had committed. The trial served the purpose of indoctrination, not of justice. Arendt views much of the trial as contributing to the very thing that Jewish people, especially those in Israel, needed to reject. Ben-Gurion and Hausner orchestrated the trial to contribute to indoctrination rather than to thinking.

At the same time, Arendt believes that the judges at the trial recognized that this was a trial of an individual. They tried to adhere to the limits of Israeli law. While Arendt believes that the judges at the trial did a good job of trying to carry out justice rather than indoctrination, she also judges the court to have failed. She writes,

> *In sum, the failure of the Jerusalem court consisted in its not coming to grips with three fundamental issues, all of which have been sufficiently well known and widely discussed since the establishment of the Nuremberg Tribunal: the problem of impaired justice in the court of the victors; a valid definition of the "crime against humanity;" and a clear recognition of the new criminal who commits this crime.* (274)

While Arendt expresses great admiration for the three judges who heard the Eichmann case, and while she agrees with the punishment determined by the judges, she believes that their final verdict did not address these issues sufficiently. In an "Epilogue" to her review of the trial, she sets out what she believes the judges should have said to Eichmann.

Arendt maintains that Eichmann's main point of defense was that when all, or almost all, are guilty, no one can be held accountable. She rejects this argument. Failure to think does not excuse a person. She says, 'in politics obedience and support are the same" (279). Eichmann's crime was to try to determine who could and who could not inhabit the world. This led him to behave in ways that suppress the sphere of appearance and that identify at least parts of humanity as superfluous. This was his crime, and this was what the judges needed to say.

The judges in the case were not trying to indoctrinate or to make law. Yet, they too, did not push thought as far as they could have. According to Arendt, they did not push it as far as they should have in order to understand most fully the experience that was before them. Most importantly, Arendt believes that the justices did not recognize the full extent of the crime that was before them. The crime before them was not simply a crime against particular people; it was a crime against humanity. She writes,

> *Had the court in Jerusalem understood that there were distinctions between discrimination, expulsion, and genocide, it would immediately have become clear that the supreme crime it was confronted with, the physical extermination of the Jewish people, was a crime against humanity, perpetrated on the body of the Jewish people, and that only the choice of victims, not the*

nature of the crime, could be derived from the long history of Jew-hatred and anti-Semitism. Insofar as the victims were Jews, it was right and proper that a Jewish court should sit in judgment; but insofar as the crime was a crime against humanity, it needed an international tribunal to do justice to it. (269)

The justices did not accept Ben-Gurion's goal of indoctrination, but their actions did not serve to open and enlarge the sphere of appearance because they could not treat the crime for what it was, an "attack on human diversity."

Facing the End of the World

Many of the objections to Arendt's analysis when it first appeared in the *New Yorker* related to her portrait of Eichmann as banal and to her challenges to the nature of the trial. However, the strongest and most harsh criticisms resulted from her analysis of the conduct of the European Jewish councils. She was called anti-Jewish and a self-hater. Given the historical proximity of her analysis to the events of the holocaust, such responses are not surprising. However, Arendt's analysis of these councils is better understood as part of an analysis of how various societies and groups of people faced the situation of which they were a part. It is also important to recognize that her report on the trial was not intended to be a complete historical account (285). Again, Arendt's analysis focuses on the importance of thinking. Her analysis suggests that where people were in the habit of thinking critically, they acted with more goodness and integrity. She develops examples from many of the European communities as well as from the Jewish Councils.

The European Communities

Because of Eichmann's direct responsibility for the deportation of Jews from many of the European countries, Arendt's analysis devotes considerable attention to the situation in various countries. She notes that there were great differences among the countries where deportation was ordered. She includes descriptions of the process of deportation from Germany, Austria, France, Belgium, Holland, Denmark, Italy,

Yugoslavia, Bulgaria, Greece, Rumania, Hungary, and Slovakia. In reading these accounts, it is helpful to remember that this is the information that was available at the time of the Eichmann trial. In her analysis of this information, Arendt tries to understand why various peoples responded so differently. She again notes the importance of a political arena and a political tradition that support critical and open exchange of ideas. Her analysis of Denmark, Bulgaria, Italy, and Romania illustrate this claim.

Arendt notes that Denmark, Sweden, Italy, and Bulgaria were the only countries that that did not exhibit anti-Semitism. However, the Danes were the only people who "dared speak out on the subject to their German masters" (171). In Denmark, the King was the first person to wear the yellow star, intended to distinguish Jews from non-Jews. The Danes refused to make the distinction between Jews of Danish origin and those who were refugees from other countries, especially Germany. When word was received that Jews were going to be seized, the Danish government informed the leaders of the Jewish community. These leaders openly informed the Jewish people and most non-Jewish Danes welcomed Jews into their homes. Because of this, most of the Jewish population was able to go into hiding. Then, with the help of Sweden, the Danes organized boats to ferry 5,919 people into Sweden (174). Because of open Danish resistance, German authorities actually worked against orders from Berlin and began to question the policy of extermination. Arendt concludes, "They had met resistance based on principle, and their 'toughness' had melted like butter in the sun, they had even been able to show a few timid beginnings of genuine courage" (175). The Danes refused to stop speaking and acting freely. They recognized that the Jewish question was really a political question. They challenged the Germans by reminding them of the possibilities of human action.

Arendt suggests that events in Bulgaria were similar to those in Denmark. The government and people of Bulgaria remained firmly committed to the Jews. The Bulgarian government openly revoked German decrees. When forced to expel all Jews from Sophia, they dispersed them into rural areas rather than concentrating them. When the Red Army approached Bulgaria in August of 1944, all anti-Jewish laws were revoked. No Bulgarian Jews were deported or died unnatural deaths. Arendt notes that she knows of no attempt to explain the action of the Bulgarians. Her implied explanation is that the Bulgarians, like the Danes, were able to make judgments between right and wrong that clearly understood human plurality in its diversity and equality.

Arendt maintains that the Danes and the Bulgarians recognized the explicitly political nature of their situation and acted on principles that acknowledged the responsibility of citizens. She judges that the Italian resistance to anti-Semitism was less conscious. It was the result of "the almost automatic general humanity of an old and civilized people" (179). Arendt describes the Italian actions as having the element of a farce. The Italians would appear to obey the German orders about clearing an area of the Jewish population, but when they arrived to carry out the order, the Jews from that region would suddenly be gone. When the Italian army left Yugoslavia, the Jews went with them. Even Mussolini participated in the farce. When pressured to introduce anti-Jewish laws, he exempted the usual groups, including people such as war veterans. However, he added a category of exemption for former members of the Fascist party and their extended families. Arendt notes that all Jewish families probably had at least one person who had been a member of the party, primarily because party-membership was a requirement for all civil service jobs. Arendt concludes that anti-Jewish measures were unpopular in Italy because Italian civilization had developed a deep sense of humanity. That sense did not fail them. She says, "Italian humanity...withstood the test of the terror that descended upon the people" (179). While they were not as openly politically reflective, they were able to call on a tradition that had developed a deep understanding of human plurality.

Romania serves to illustrate the responses of a people who did not have this sense of humanity and who did not think about the responsibilities of citizenship. In Romania, citizens were so anti-Semitic that they slaughtered Jews in spontaneous pogroms. The SS intervened in order to carry out killing in "a more civilized way" (190). Romania joined the war on the side of Hitler under the leadership of Marshal Ion Antonescu. Antonescu led the way in depriving Jews of citizenship and in exterminating Jews. He also was the first to begin trading Jews for money. This resulted in Romania becoming a path for Jewish emigration to Palestine. But this possibility for safety was not established out of political understanding or out of a tradition of humanity. Arendt maintains that it was because Rumania was not only a country of murders; it was also corrupt.

Arendt develops this account of the responses in these and other European countries to explain Eichmann's role in each country. However, her analysis also clearly shows that where people saw the situation as requiring political or human response, there was resistance to the German atrocities. Where there was no such political thought, terror and genocide occurred.

The Jewish Councils

While there are only a few pages in *Eichmann in Jerusalem* that address the role of the Jewish leadership, Arendt's remarks on this issue generated tremendous controversy. She was accused of alleging that the Jews were responsible for their deaths either because they had not resisted or because their leadership had betrayed them. While she does think that the role of Jewish leadership is a serious question, she maintains that her analysis does not condemn the Jewish Councils. She tries to detach her analysis from the emotional context and look at the facts of the situation, especially in the context of Eichmann's relationship to those facts. Arendt's main point seems to be that the Jewish Councils did not draw a distinction between "helping Jews to emigrate and helping the Nazis to deport them" (284). This helped Eichmann to carry out the deportation of Jews. She recounts the role of Jewish police in Berlin in rounding up Jews for deportation. She acknowledges that Jewish leaders kept the truth from people in order to prevent people from panicking, but she questions the real humanity of this silence.

Arendt maintains that facts show that many people might have been saved if they had not followed the instructions of the Jewish Councils. She writes,

> *Wherever Jews lived, there were recognized Jewish leaders, and this leadership, almost without exception, cooperated in one way or another, for one reason or another, with the Nazis. The whole truth was that if the Jewish people had really been unorganized and leaderless, there would have been chaos and plenty of misery but the total number of victims would hardly have been between four and a half and six million people.* (125)

Arendt's point is not to blame the Jewish leadership for Eichmann's crimes. Rather, she includes what she understands to be factual information about the role of the Jewish Councils because it confirms that Eichmann did not hear opposition to the Final Solution, even from the Jewish leadership.

She also includes the information because she believes that it is vital to a full understanding of the events and the trial did not present this information in a clear manner. She recognizes that the prosecution had good reason for not discussing the activities of the Jewish

Councils. It would have worked against the claim that Eichmann himself made the deportation lists. The defense would normally have brought this evidence forward, but the defense was silent on this issue. Arendt believes that a full understanding of the holocaust requires that the role of the Councils be acknowledged and thoughtfully considered.

Her account of Jewish leadership also notes that there was Jewish resistance by a "tiny minority." She comments that she found the testimony of a member of the resistance welcome because "It dissipated the haunting specter of universal cooperation, the stifling, poisoned atmosphere which had surrounded the Final solution" (123). Arendt's unemotional analysis again recognizes the importance of action, of resistance to the forces that threaten to destroy humanity.

The Problem of Human Judgment

In the "Postscript" to *Eichmann in Jerusalem*, Arendt identifies a fundamental problem that she believes is presented in all of the postwar trials, especially in the trial of Eichmann. This is a moral problem having to do with human judgment. How is it that humans can tell right from wrong? Certainly, the case of Eichmann suggests that human instinct is not sufficient. Moreover, human societies develop rules that work against good judgment and clichés that enable individuals to avoid making responsible judgments. Arendt notes that those people who were still able to distinguish right from wrong "went really only by their own judgments" (295). Again, her analysis points to the fragility of what is most fully human while at the same time offering hope that even in the darkest times, human freedom is possible.

5

Facing Dark Times

Hannah Arendt adopted the concept of "dark times" from the poem, "To Posterity," by Bertolt Brecht. He writes, "You who will emerge from the flood in which we drowned remember when you speak of our weaknesses the dark time from which you escaped" (224). For Arendt, the dark times are primarily the twentieth century and the totalitarianism and bureaucracy that dominate the period and diminish the public realm. However, she acknowledges that dark times are not new to human existence, but occur whenever the public realm is threatened. It is the function of the public realm to be a sphere of appearance and so shed light or illuminate human existence and human affairs. She writes,

> Darkness has come when this light is extinguished by "credibility gaps" and "invisible government," by speech that does not disclose what is but sweeps it under the carpet, by exhortations, moral and otherwise, that, under the pretext of upholding old truths, degrade all truth to meaningless triviality. (viii)

Yet, she maintains that even in the darkest of times there is the possibility of illumination. In keeping with her emphasis on the importance of human experience and action, she maintains that this illumination is most likely to come from the lives of individual women and men. The stories of these individuals help make human meaning intelligible.

Storytelling

Arendt is concerned to think about the political, but she is hesitant about developing a political theory. Perhaps because she is so aware of human frailty and the possibility of dark times, she believes that narrative is more able to help us think about our experiences than is theory. Stories help all humans find meaning and help us find that meaning together in our plurality.

In *The Human Condition,* Arendt explains the importance of storytelling in relationship to action. Stories arise out of human plurality, out of what Arendt calls the web of human relationships. She describes this web as consisting of conflicting wills and intentions. Because of this, stories are not the work of an individual person. She says that they have no author. Rather, stories reveal an agent. She says of a story, "Somebody began it and is its subject in the twofold sense of the word, namely, its actor and sufferer, but nobody is its author" (184). Fictional stories do have authors, but they are invented. In contrast, real stories are experienced and arise out of action and passion. Stories imitate acting and speaking in order to convey meaning. Because of this imitation, stories can often only be told after the actors are dead. The storyteller finds the meaning in the action. Arendt says, "Even though stories are the inevitable results of action, it is not the actor but the storyteller who perceives and 'makes' the story" (192).

A story appears to many people, not simply to the actor in the story. Stories enable people to speak and act together and to appear to each other. In *Men in Dark Times*, Arendt includes a chapter on Isak Dinesen, the author of *Out of Africa*. She says of Dinesen, that stories saved her life. "The story reveals the meaning of what otherwise would remain an unbearable sequence of sheer happenings" (104). Stories can disclose meaning without confining that meaning to set definitions. Although each person's life may contain a story, no one can live her or his life as a story. Someone else who can recollect and repeat the story in imagination must tell each story. This recollection and repetition hold people together in a community of distinct and unique individuals. We can only tell the other's story, not our own. In telling these stories, we come to understand human existence. In telling stories, people are also loyal to life. That is, they show themselves to be worthy of life by pondering life.

In *Men in Dark Times*, Arendt functions as a storyteller and so emphasizes that the role of the political historian, and perhaps also of the philosopher, is to be a storyteller. She gathers together accounts of

56

the actions of ten people, many of whom were her friends. By telling their stories, she is loyal to these people. Telling their stories also enables her to acknowledge the meaningfulness of these lives. She says, "the meaning of a committed act is revealed only when the action itself has come to an end and become a story susceptible to narration" (21). In developing her narratives she also emphasizes the importance of reconciliation to what life gives. Human stories are not fictions that distort the realities of life; rather, stories provide meaning with permanence, with a possibility of survival. The book contains some of her most powerful writing as she tells the stories of Lessing, Luxemburg, Pope John XXIII, Jaspers, Dinesen, Broch, Benjamin, Brecht, Gurian, and Jarrell. In each case, she focuses on the light that each person kindled to help us understand human existence. The stories of these people disclose possibilities for achieving humanness, even in dark times.

Lessing and Friendship

The first essay in *Men in Dark Times* is titled "On Humanity in Dark Times: Thoughts about Lessing." The essay was first given as a public address in 1959 when Arendt was awarded the Lessing Prize by the city of Hamburg, Germany. Gotthold Lessing (1729-81) had lived in Hamburg and the Lessing Prize was established in his memory to celebrate Enlightenment humanism and the values of freedom and tolerance. In offering the prize to Arendt, a Jew, the city of Hamburg was trying to facilitate a process of reconciliation. Yet, the prize was offered to her not as a Jew, but as a humanist. In giving the address, Arendt is concerned to raise this issue in a way that can result in thoughtful consideration rather than difficult feelings. Her approach is to reflect on Lessing and on his understanding of friendship.

Arendt begins by noting that Lessing lived in times that were dark. In such times, it is tempting for people to retreat into isolated thought, to emigrate into the self. According to Arendt, Lessing recognized that such retreat results in loss to the world. She uses her understanding of the world as the public sphere that is located between people to explain this loss. She says, "what is lost is the specific and usually irreplaceable in-between which should have formed between this individual and his fellow men" (4-5). In Lessing, Arendt finds an example of a person who elects to think without retreating into the safety of the isolated self. She writes,

> *For Lessing, thought does not arise out of the individual and is not the manifestation of a self. Rather, the individual – whom Lessing would say was created for action, not ratiocination – elects such thought because he discovers in thinking another mode of moving in the world of freedom.* (9)

For Lessing, friendship is fundamental for moving in the realm of freedom and thus for thinking.

Arendt finds in Lessing an important distinction between friendship and fraternity. Fraternity involves the sharing of suffering and arises among the exploited and oppressed. It results in strong feelings of warmth and attachment, but these feelings are not easily transferred to those who do not share in the particular sufferings. Friendship is a sharing of joy and discourse, sometimes in the midst of persecution, but not because of it. Arendt illustrates this claim with the example of friendship between a German and a Jew under the conditions of the Third Reich. She believes that such friendship could not ignore the political situation and so could not be based on their common humanness. They would need to acknowledge that they were a German and a Jew who were friends. But, she says, where such friendship succeeded "a bit of humanness in a world become inhuman had been achieved" (23). Friendship becomes a form of resistance and so an illumination of meaningful human existence.

Arendt emphasizes that Lessing makes it clear that "friendship is not intimately personal but makes political demands and preserves reference to the world" (25). In friendship, the world is the object of discourse. Friendship is not concerned with agreement and sharing one truth. Friendship takes place between people and so holds open a space of human plurality and difference. Lessing illuminates the human world by showing that no doctrine is worth the sacrifice of friendship. She says that for Lessing, "Any doctrine that in principle barred the possibility of friendship between two human beings would have been rejected" (29). In dark times, friendship allows each person to speak what he or she takes to be true. This helps preserve human plurality and so a world where human existence is possible. Telling the story of Lessing enables Arendt to grasp the importance of friendship for human existence. It also enables her to respond to the receipt of the Lessing Prize in a manner that both respects and challenges those who awarded the prize.

Jaspers and Limitless Communication

Karl Jaspers, Arendt's teacher and mentor is probably also the source of her example of friendship between a German and a Jew. *Men in Dark Times* include two chapters on Jaspers. The first, "Karl Jaspers: A Laudatio," is a public address, given in 1958 when Jaspers was awarded the German Peace Prize. The second, "Karl Jaspers: Citizen of the World?" was originally written for a volume on Jaspers and his philosophical thought.

Arendt deeply respected Jaspers for his conduct during and after World War II. While Arendt agonized over giving the address in praise of Jaspers just as she had over giving the address for the Lessing Prize, it provided her with the opportunity to publicly acknowledge Jaspers and so to confirm his commitment to the public nature of reason. Jaspers' thought before the War had emphasized the importance of reasoning, not as a solitary activity, but as an exchange between people. Reasoning together, people create a space in which they can live together. She writes of Jaspers,

> *What distinguishes Jaspers is that he is more at home in this region of reason and freedom, knows his way about it with greater sureness, than others who may be acquainted with it but cannot endure living constantly in it. Because his existence was governed by the passion for light itself, he was able to be like a light in the darkness glowing from some hidden source of luminosity.* (76)

Arendt maintains that because Jaspers was so at home in this space opened by reason, he was able to lead others into this region and so help them recognize their mutual humanity.

In the second piece on Jaspers, Arendt examines what he means by world citizenship. She is concerned that the development of technology could result in a world where there is unity that is dogmatic, excluding the human plurality which she believes is so fundamental for human existence. This would serve to push people further into dark times. She believes that Jaspers' emphasis on limitless communication provides a way of thinking about world citizenship that presents technological advances as a beginning, rather than an end, for humanity.

Limitless communication means that truth can only be conceived through constant communication. Truth cannot be established or proven once and for all. Humans keep a tradition alive through communication and through such communication truth is disclosed. In the process of such communication, humans can overcome what is dogmatic in their thought and ways of life and "retain only what is universally communicative" (90). This does not mean that what remains is a single, rigid framework. People communicating with each other as Jaspers suggests will not abolish cultural and individual differences. Rather, this communication will enable people to take joy in living in the midst of such difference. Jaspers' understanding of communication leads him to see light in the dark times and so to hope that we stand before a door that will open onto new possibilities rather than remain closed. Arendt does not judge Jaspers to be Utopian in this hope because his life stands as an example of the possibility of limitless communication.

Broch and Human Helpfulness

Arendt met the poet and novelist Hermann Broch in 1946 shortly before she began working for the publisher, Schocken. They became good friends, and she held his work in high esteem. She believed that he, like Jaspers, understood that the period in which they lived was one of ending and beginning. It was a period of uncertainty between what had been in the nineteenth century and what was not yet clear. A collection of her essays named this the time *Between Past and Future.* She believed that Broch's work tried to deal with the emptiness of twentieth-century experience. After Broch's death in 1951, Arendt organized his papers and wrote an introduction to two volumes of his essays. This is included in *Men in Dark Times* with the simple title, "Herman Broch, 1886 – 1951."

While Arendt judged Broch to be much greater as a poet than as a philosopher, her introduction is written to his more philosophical work. Arendt explains that Broch's thought and life were concerned with the unity of human existence. Like the other individuals that Arendt identifies as illuminating dark times, Broch clearly understood that any human unity has to respect and preserve human plurality and uniqueness. She describes Broch as living within a triangle of literature, knowledge, and action. He demanded that literature "possess the same compelling validity as science," that science present a vision that summons the world in the same way as art, and that both "should comprehend and include" the practical activities of human existence (112). Arendt notes that within the context of the life of one person, this demand must lead to conflicts and that Broch experienced such conflict. She notes that the demand that Broch placed on himself to live this unity had tremendous consequences for his practical life. He lived a constantly interrupted life of human helpfulness. She writes,

> *Whenever an acquaintance – not just a friend, which would have kept things within reasonable limits, but any acquaintance – was in distress, was sick or had no money or was dying, it was Broch who took care of everything.* (113)

It was in the demands of action that he found a living unity for life in such uncertain times.

Elisabeth Young-Bruehl, in her biography of Arendt, maintains that Arendt's true opinion of Broch was that he was a much poorer philosopher than literary writer (196). However, in the essay printed in *Men in Dark Times*, Arendt highlights some of the important points of the epistemological and metaphysical thought contained in Broch's essays. For example, she outlines his understanding of time and space where time is understood as the sense by which the world is given to us internally. She understands the implication of this understanding of time for his theory of music as the transformation of time into space. She also explains what Broch called the earthly absolute and its connection to his theory of time. However, Young-Bruehl is correct. Arendt is not so interested in the importance of the particular concepts that Broch developed as in his life-long emphasis on the need to think those things which are closest to human existence and which, therefore, may be "most alien and menacing" (141).

At the end of her essay, Arendt returns to the importance of human helpfulness, not only for Broch's life, but also for his thought. His epistemological and metaphysical thought showed him the importance of redemption for human existence. This redemption was possible, not because of an act of a transcendent God, but because humans, in their daily relationships, can act in accordance with the "imperativeness of the claim for help" (150). In the end, the meaning illuminated by Broch's life was this ethical imperative. Arendt reports that he took this imperative so much for granted that he did not think it had to be demonstrated. Like Jaspers, Broch lived a life that sheds light on what is most meaningful for human existence.

Benjamin and Human Connection

Arendt's essay on Walter Benjamin, included in *Men in Dark Times*, first appeared in 1968 in the *New Yorker*. The essay is a beautiful tribute to a friend who did not manage to escape the holocaust. Benjamin's own writing was often in response to friendship, for he held that friends raise questions that deserve answers. Arendt's essay narrates Benjamin's life, presenting and addressing the question that his life raises: How, in the face of our break with the past, can we find new ways of dealing with the past? How can we establish a human connection with the past that presents us with possibilities for a new future?

Benjamin understood himself to be a literary critic. To him, this identity meant that he was responsible for illuminating literary works, not for commenting on these works. Arendt says that he understood a critic to be

> *An alchemist practicing the obscure art of transmuting the futile elements of the real into the shining, enduring gold of truth, or rather watching and interpreting the historical process that brings about such magical transfiguration...* (157)

The critic's role is to gather things together so that they can illuminate each other and human existence. She notes that Benjamin's propensity for collection contributed to his role as a critic. It led him to a great insight about the function of the past in the present.

Benjamin gathered the scraps from the tradition and placed them together in order to illumine human existence. Arendt observes that "Benjamin had a passion for small, even minute things" (163). He was interested in phenomena, rather than in ideas. He was a passionate collector. Arendt maintains that a collector, such as Benjamin was, levels difference. The collector destroys the context of the thing collected and places it in a new context, next to other things collected. Rather than preserving the past, the collector places things together that then have the possibility of generating fresh meaning.

Arendt maintains that Benjamin's tendency to collect leads him to recognize the importance of metaphor. Metaphor holds things together and establishes a connection that does not need further interpretation. Because of the new connections that arise in metaphor, metaphors enable us to see and to understand in a new way what has always been there.

Arendt explains how his passion for collecting small things also helped Benjamin to discover the "modern function of quotations" (193). Quotations do not function to preserve the past in its authority. Rather, the way in which Benjamin uses quotation demonstrates that citations have a destructive capability. They are torn out of the past and positioned in order to provide hope. In their new position, they help to cleanse the past. She says that Benjamin's most important works "consisted in tearing fragments out of their context and arranging them afresh in such a way that they illustrated one another" (202).

His work points to the importance of language and of what she calls, in accord with Heidegger, "the gift of thinking poetically." This thinking delves into the past, "not in order to resuscitate it the way it was and to contribute to the renewal of extinct ages," but in order to bring forward thought fragments that can present the present with possibilities (205). Thinking poetically helps humans make new connections that provide the possibility of transfiguring human existence.

Luxemburg and Revolution

The chapter on Rosa Luxemburg was written as a review of J. P. Nettl's biography of Rosa Luxemburg. It first appeared in *The New York Review of Books* in 1966. Arendt's mother introduced her to the importance of Luxemburg as a political thinker in 1919, when she admonished her daughter to take note of the importance of the Spartacists. Arendt's later reflections on Luxemburg confirm her mother's opinion of the importance of Luxemburg as an individual.

Arendt emphasizes that Luxemburg was always "out of step" with others. As a Marxist she was not orthodox, nor was she polemical. Arendt evaluates Luxemburg as being interested in Marx because of his keen insight into reality. Arendt says, "What mattered most in her view was reality, in all its wonderful and all its frightful aspects, even more than revolution itself" (39). It was not Marxist theory that gripped Luxemburg. She was a Socialist because of her insights into the realities of her experience.

Arendt also notes the importance of moral motivation for Luxemburg. She praises Nettl for discovering the importance of Luxemburg's connection to the Polish-Jewish peer group. This group consisted of assimilated Jews who had German cultural backgrounds, but who were influenced by Russian political thought. They were held together by a shared ethical code. Arendt says of this group,

> *What the members of the peer group had in common was what can only be called moral taste, which is so different from "moral principles"; the authenticity of their morality they owed to having grown up in a world that was not out of joint.* (41)

The revolutionary spirit of this group was based in their moral insight.

Arendt maintains that Luxemburg was able to recognize her own errors and the errors of revolution because she was always morally motivated and reflected out of her experience. Arendt notes that Luxemburg was at times in agreement with the German Social Democratic Party, and that she came to recognize her agreement as mistaken. The example of Luxemburg's relationship to what is known as the revisionist controversy is especially significant according to Arendt. This controversy concerned whether the German Party should support reform as an alternative to revolution. Luxemburg was initially supportive of the Party position to continue to advocate revolution. However, she came to recognize that her motivation for supporting revolution was not the same as the motivation of the Party's leadership. Arendt maintains that the Party leaders opposed reform because "the Party had in fact become a huge and well-organized bureaucracy that stood outside society and had every interest in things as they were" (49). They advocated revolution out of a foundation in theory and in order to maintain party growth. Luxemburg also advocated revolution, but she was motivated by moral principles and by her experiences of reality. Luxemburg was not interested in being part of a cadre. Arendt maintains that her moral motivations kept her "passionately engaged in public life and civil affairs" (51). It led her to insist on the importance of a republican program, on the importance of public freedom. Arendt admires Luxemburg for standing alone and refusing to accept a victory that did not give people in general a role and a voice. In Luxemburg, Arendt finds a kindred spirit, someone who clearly recognized the importance of the political sphere as a place of speech and action for all citizens.

Arendt sees illuminated in Luxemburg's life the importance of experience over theory and the importance of moral motivation for political action. When humans act out of the experience of a healthy moral world, they are far more likely to act to promote a human world. Acting out of theory is likely to lead humans into error. Luxemburg lived a life that revealed both the limitations of theory and the importance of moral experience.

Holding Open the Possibility of New Beginnings

The essays on Lessing, Jaspers, Broch, Benjamin, and Luxemburg, as well as the other essays in *Men in Dark Times*, all emphasize the importance of individual human lives for making possible what is most human in life. Arendt's understanding of human plurality emphasizes that each life is a new beginning. Each life is capable of presenting the human world with new possibilities for existence. While Arendt does not minimize the horror of the dark times of the twentieth century, she believes that these stories of individual lives present us with possibilities for new beginnings as we move into the future. Lives that illuminate friendship, limitless communication, human helpfulness, human connection and the importance of thinking from experience rather than theory hold open the hope and possibility of new beginnings for all of human existence.

6

Reflections on American Experience

Hannah Arendt identified a significant hope for humanity in the American Republic, which she embraced as her new home. While she was uncomfortable with much of what she identified as American society, she saw the American political structure as an exciting possibility. Much of her writing during the 1960s focused on the struggles of the Republic and the possibilities that she saw in the American political structure. As with her earlier writing, she did not conceal the problems that she believed were present in the American political sphere. However, she continued to find ways of illuminating problems and identifying hopeful directions and possibilities. *On Revolution* and *Crises of the Republic* provide insight into her understanding and critique of the American Republic.

On Revolution

On Revolution was published shortly after *Eichmann in Jerusalem*. Because of the controversy surrounding the book on Eichmann, *On Revolution* did not receive a great deal of immediate attention. Karl Jaspers struggled through it in English and wrote Arendt on May 16,

1963,

> *I think it is a book that is the equal of, if not perhaps superior to, your book on totalitarianism in the profundity of its political outlook... You will have made historical discoveries here that will rouse the Americans out of their self-forgetfulness.... Ultimately, the whole is your vision of a tragedy that does not leave you despairing: an element of the tragedy of humankind.* (Letter 327)

Jaspers recognized that *On Revolution* was a warning of the importance of preserving what was best in the American Revolution. Arendt believed that what was politically important was to preserve freedom in the face of authoritarianism. She believed that Americans were wrong to believe that the international conflict was over economic, rather than political, structures.

In her analysis of revolution, Arendt focused on the French and American revolutions. She observed that the French Revolution was the revolution that has been considered most historically important. Even today, history texts take the French revolution as an important dividing line in Western history. Yet, Arendt maintains that the American Revolution was much more successful.

Both revolutions preferred "public freedom to civil liberties or public happiness to private welfare" (134). However, the American Revolution did not restrict civil rights as the French Revolution did. Both revolutions recognized that the aim of revolution was really the "constitution of freedom." In America, constitution writing was part of the Revolution in all of the colonies. Arendt observes that fighting and constitution writing "altogether different stages of the revolutionary process began at almost the same moment and continued to run parallel to each other all through the years of war""(141).

Arendt believes that the American experience of revolution revealed that real power resides in the people. She makes use of the distinction between power and authority that she develops in her writings on violence. Power belongs to people as groups. These people bestow authority. The Americans recognized that revolution was not about the establishment of power, but rather of authority. They recognized that power resides in the people who then bestow authority. They had power. The task was to bestow authority. Arendt maintains that the American Revolution was not a result of an outbreak of violence. Rather, it "was made by men in common deliberation and on the strength of mutual pledges" (213). People were combined through the process of deliberation and by their mutual promises.

Arendt observes that Thomas Jefferson learned from the experience of revolution that included constitution writing. He believed that the Constitution should be revised at regular intervals, because each generation has a right to choose its own form of government. Arendt believes that Jefferson recognized that the actions of establishing government through writing a constitution were the activities that "constituted the space of freedom" (235).

Arendt believed that Jefferson's insight into the need for ongoing revolution was the "lost treasure" of revolution. This insight emphasized the importance of the experience of writing the constitution. This constitution-making experience institutes and preserves public space. What he recognized was the importance of every member of society having the possibility of participating in public affairs. This does not mean that everyone would participate. But those "from all walks of life who have a taste for public freedom and cannot be 'happy' without it" would be able to create and participate in a public realm (279). She believes that the insight of the importance of this opportunity for participation was "buried in the disasters of twentieth-century revolutions" (265). The possibility of a system of councils that would give all citizens this participatory possibility has not happened in the twentieth century. Yet, Arendt believes that it is still the best possibility for addressing the problems presented by modern mass society.

On Revolution was read in the 1960s, particularly by students who were interested in political issues and by those involved in the free speech movements on campuses across the United States. Most of these readers embraced the idea of grassroots participatory democracy and supported the importance of council systems. However, most rejected her critique of society and thought her emphasis on revolution as primarily concerned with constitution writing to be limited. Arendt's warning, contained in the book, about the importance of preserving human freedom rather than working to change economic systems, was not widely heard.

Crises of the Republic

Crises of the Republic is a collection of essays originally written for the *New Yorker* and *The New York Review of Books*. These essays address the major challenges of the 1960s and 1970s to the American Republic. They also emphasize the importance of citizen participation for the health and preservation of a vital American Republic. Arendt discusses the Pentagon Papers and the danger of deceit for political life, the role of civil disobedience in the American Republic, and the risks to human freedom inherent in violence. Her analyses continue to emphasize the importance for human existence of thinking what we are doing.

Lying

In June of 1971, the New York *Times* published secret documents, commissioned by Secretary of Defense Robert S. McNamara. These documents, which contained a history of the decision-making process related to the United States involvement in Vietnam, became known as the Pentagon Papers. Arendt, like many other readers of these papers, recognized that these papers raise many questions about deception in the political sphere. She focused on this deception in "Lying in Politics."

In beginning her analysis, Arendt affirms her belief in freedom. Human action can change the world. It can begin something new. This means, however, that lies are also possible human actions and that human freedom is vulnerable to lies. In addition, lies are easily accepted because they have to do with matters of fact, and people recognize that factual claims are contingent. Facts are never without the possibility of doubt, and so, they are always fragile. This fragility makes lying more possible. Arendt writes,

> *Lies are often much more plausible, more appealing to reason, than reality, since the liar has the great advantage of knowing beforehand what the audience wishes or expects to hear. ... whereas reality has the disconcerting habit of confronting us with the unexpected, for which we were not prepared.* (6-7)

Arendt notes that humans have developed many types of lies. Some of these are quickly and easily defeated by reality. However, some types of lies totally remove truth from human existence and destabilize and destroy human freedom.

Arendt suggests that two related ways of lying have recently developed. She makes the strong claim that the first type of lying is public relations. Public relations is a form of advertising that manipulates facts in order to get people to consume, to buy things. In the political arena, those in public relations manipulate the facts in order to get people to buy certain political candidates and views. Public relations is concerned with creating images and then getting people to accept those images as reality. Arendt notes that this form of lying was used in the strategy surrounding Vietnam. Many involved in the decision making related to the Vietnam War were concerned to sell the United States as the most powerful superpower. How to sell the war to the American public was also an important consideration. However, Arendt emphasizes that the American public did not completely "buy" the image that was sold. Because other information was available to the American people, at least some were able to recognize that the image that was being created about the war did not fit the reality of the facts.

Arendt identifies professional problem solving as the second newly developed form of lying. It is this type of lying that Arendt believes played a greater role in the decision-making process about Vietnam. Arendt believes that this type of lying is particularly problematic because the people who engage in it are basically good, well-educated people. She finds the weakness of such people in their love of theory. She maintains that the love of theory leads them to be impatient with facts. She says that problem solvers are easily tempted to make the facts fit a theory. In forcing the facts, they rid themselves of the "disconcerting contingency" of reality (12).

Arendt illustrates her claim about theory with the example of the domino theory. This theory held that if Vietnam became communist, the whole of Southeast Asia would quickly fall to communism, like a row of dominoes. Arendt notes that the Pentagon Papers show that as early as 1964, President Johnson was aware that such a domino effect was highly unlikely. Yet, he and many others continued to use the theory, "not merely for public statement, but as part of their own premises as well" (25).

Arendt's analysis points out two important aspects of this form of lying. It starts with self-deception. The decision-makers lived in what Arendt calls a defactualized world. Because they began with theories, it was easy for them to ignore facts and it was easy for them to ignore those who were not convinced. They could ignore those who opposed the war because they were firmly convinced by their theories that they would win both the war and the public relations campaign. They did not need to listen to other voices. Moreover, this form of lying relies on calculation rather than judgment. Arendt believes that the problem solvers behaved more like gamblers than statespeople. They were unwilling to consult and learn from reality. They relied on theories and images that removed them from the realities of the situation.

Arendt's analysis does not minimize the threat to American democracy represented by the actions of those in government. However, she ends her analysis of the Pentagon Papers on a hopeful note. There was very little in the massive volume of papers, despite their secret classification, that the American people did not already know. The press had served the people well. She writes, "so long as the press is free and not corrupt, it has an enormously important function to fulfill and can rightly be called the fourth branch of government" (45). Moreover, she notes that there is something about the American people's character that resists the destruction of freedom. Even in the face of the crisis of a war that Arendt agreed was misguided, she takes hope in the character of the American people.

Civil Disobedience

Crises of the Republic also includes an essay on civil disobedience. While Arendt considers civil disobedience to be a crisis for the Republic, she understands civil disobedience as a positive challenge for the Republic. While civil disobedience may turn to violence and so have some of the same destructive capabilities as lying, it also identifies an important moral obligation for citizens in a society established by consent.

Arendt recognizes the importance of civil disobedience for both the American civil rights movement and the movement against the war in Vietnam. Although it is possible to use Socrates as an example of a civil disobedient, Arendt believes civil disobedience is primarily an American phenomenon. She maintains that the issue of civil disobedience arises out of the citizen's moral responsibility to the law in a society of consent. The United States is the country that has named this phenomenon, and "is the only government having at least a chance to cope with it…in accordance with the *spirit* of its laws" (83). Her essay encourages the United States to consider ways of incorporating civil disobedience into its legal system.

She distinguishes civil disobedience from conscientious objection. While a single individual can object to a government law or policy on the basis of conscience, civil disobedience requires that one be a member of a group. She maintains that those who engage in civil disobedience are members of organized groups that are held together by a common opinion and take a stand together against the government.

71

She writes, "their concerted action springs from an agreement with each other, and it is this agreement that lends credence and conviction to their opinion, no matter how they may originally have arrived at it" (56). They recognize that while they belong to a society of consent, their consent is contingent on the right to dissent.

Civil disobedience is not an act of revolution. Those who engage in civil disobedience accept the general structure and legitimacy of the legal system. Yet, both revolutionaries and those who engage in civil disobedience want to change the world. The results of civil disobedience can sometimes be similar to the results of revolution, as is demonstrated by Gandhi. However, civil disobedience is based on consent, on "active support and continuing participation in all matters of public interest" (85).

Because dissent is so vital to a society based on consent, Arendt proposes that the United States needs to provide a constitutional niche for civil disobedience. This is especially important because many forms of voluntary association have diminished. She sees a crisis precipitated by loss of citizen participation rather than by the participation in civil disobedience. She writes,

> *Representative government itself is in crisis today, partly because it has lost, in the course of time, all institutions that permitted the citizens' actual participation, and partly because it is now gravely affected by the disease from which the party system suffers: bureaucratization and the two parties' tendency to represent nobody except the party machines.* (89)

Those who engage in civil disobedience form the voluntary associations that are vital to the American experience.

Indeed, Arendt maintains that, as the newest form of voluntary association, the groups formed in the 1960s to engage in civil disobedience are part of the oldest tradition of voluntary associations in the United States. Moreover, they are associations based on moral principles rather than on self-interest. While there may be difficulties involved in incorporating actions of civil disobedience into the American legal code, Arendt believes that it should be attempted. She believes that such voluntary associations are the peculiar "American remedy for the failure of institutions" (102). Civil disobedience may well be a means that enables the United States with some confidence of its ability to preserve human freedom.

Violence

"On Violence" was originally published as a separate essay, but is, very appropriately, included in *Crises of the Republic*. In treating violence, she notes that, despite the role that violence has played in human history, it has seldom been treated directly. She believes that this lack of attention, "shows to what an extent violence and its arbitrariness were taken for granted and therefore neglected; no one questions or examines what is obvious to all" (110). Arendt maintains that what seems so obvious about violence is more complicated upon closer consideration. In writing about violence, Arendt uses the phenomenological approach that she developed and relied on for most of her analyses. She begins in the context of experience and from her great wealth of historical and philosophical knowledge. She avoids theory and tries to describe political realities in order to understand the sorts of actions that may be most helpful for developing political arenas where all people can speak and act freely.

The student movements of the 1960s stimulated Arendt's reflections on violence. She is concerned that the "Marxist rhetoric of the New Left coincides with the steady growth of the entirely non-Marxian conviction, proclaimed by Mao Tse-tung, that 'Power grows out of the barrel of a gun'" (113). Yet, she recognizes that these same groups, which often preach violence, are motivated by moral considerations. Indeed she maintains that the student rebellions are "almost exclusively motivated by moral considerations" (130). Arendt questions why these students do not understand that their rhetoric of violence is incompatible with their moral motivations.

In addressing this question, Arendt distinguishes among power, strength, force, authority, and violence. She has developed and used some of these distinctions in her previous writing. For example, in *The Human Condition*, her understanding of power is very important to her analysis of human action. She identifies power as belonging to a group. It is the human ability to "act in concert." Strength, on the other hand, is a characteristic of individuals. She believes that force is not the same as violence, but should be used to identify "forces released by physical or social movements" (143). Authority, according to Arendt is illusive. It is bestowed and so has its origin in respect. She believes that violence, like strength, has an instrumental character. These distinctions lead her to the conclusion that violence is not a form of power but rather the opposite of power.

She concludes that violence can destroy, but can never create power. Violence is not irrational, but is a form of action that is able to change the world. She again calls on the insight developed in *The Human Condition*, that actions are irreversible and unpredictable. Violence, once begun, cannot be controlled. What experience shows is that the most likely result of violent action is "a more violent world" (177). Power, on the other hand, is more likely to result in a world that respects plurality and that makes possible the sorts of political structures that preserve the political sphere for free speaking and acting. This is the insight that she hopes to convey to the student movements.

Their moral motivations indicate that, even when they espouse the use of violence, they are acting in a manner that is more correctly understood as power. They act together in the public arena, motivated by moral principles. While she finds hope in this movement, she also recognizes the temptation to substitute violence for power (184). When a group or a government find power slipping away, it is easy to try to hold onto power by means of violence. Arendt believes that it is important to remember that this is not possible. When violence appears, power is clearly in jeopardy (155).

Vision of a Council-State

In 1970, Arendt gave an interview to the German writer, Adelbert Reif. Much of the interview focused on the essay "On Violence." While Arendt never presented a political theory that advocated specific state structures, she continued to believe, as she had suggested in *On Revolution*, that the greatest hope for the preservation of the American Republic was in a council system. In that interview she reiterated this belief. She concluded the interview with the following statement,

> *In this direction I see the possibility of forming a new concept of the state. A council-state of this sort, to which the principle of sovereignty would be wholly alien, would be admirably suited to federations of the most various kinds, especially because in it power would be constituted horizontally and not vertically.* (233)

While she could envision such a state, and even hope for it, she also thought that the prospects of such a council-state emerging were very slight.

7

The Significance of
Thought

Because of the circumstances of her life, Arendt's early inclinations towards a contemplative life were interrupted by demands for action, for living a life in the political arena. In spite of her political focus, she claimed that her main form of activity was thinking, and that she could not claim to be a person of action as others could. She was not a revolutionary or a member of the resistance. Yet, her thinking was constantly interrupted by the need to think about the political. In the last years of her life, she consciously tried to provide herself with the time and solitude to think about thinking. Even then, she was interrupted by what she experienced as the urgency of political events. She wrote "Lying in Politics," in response to the Pentagon Papers during this period. However, she did manage to think and write about thinking in the last few years of her life.

Thinking and Moral Considerations

Arendt delivered the lecture "Thinking and Moral Considerations" the day before Heinrich Blücher died. This lecture is an excellent introduction to her work on thinking. She begins, "To talk about thinking seems to me…presumptuous" (417). She recognizes that she may be trying to do something that she cannot, or should not do. She recognizes the possibilities that such thought is not possible or that it is more important for her to continue her political analyses. She returns to her reflections on Eichmann to discern a justification for thinking about thinking.

She reflects on the experience of the trial and remembers that it was Eichmann's "total absence of thinking" that struck her. She notes that it was during this trial that she began to ask if the human ability to judge is dependent on the ability to think. A question imposed itself on her.

Could the activity of thinking as such, the habit of examining and reflecting upon whatever happens to come to pass, regardless of specific content and quite independent of results, could this activity be of such a nature that it "conditions" men against evil-doing? (418)

Clearly, her reflections on dark times as well as her analysis of the events of the holocaust led her to suspect the connection between thinking and actions of conscience. Yet, in this important lecture, Arendt seems to be publicly struggling with the question of whether or not it is philosophically permissible for her to think about thinking. In the lecture she wrestles with herself and finds a justification for the thought that results in her final and incomplete work, *The Life of the Mind*.

Thinking and Knowing

Arendt's first struggle in the lecture is with the possibility that asking a question such as "What is thinking?" is to engage in metaphysics and so, perhaps, to engage in a form of philosophy that is dead. She knows that after Nietzsche and after the emergence of positivism in philosophy, traditional metaphysical questions are themselves highly questionable. Yet, she maintains that the modern deaths of metaphysics, and even of positivism, are themselves "thought events." Indeed, she concludes that humans have an inclination, and even a need, to think. This means that humans are pushed to do more than use their intellectual abilities "for knowing and doing." Humans "think beyond the limitations of knowledge" (421).

Arendt calls on the distinction that Kant makes between thinking and knowing and maintains that this distinction is crucial for her own understanding. Kant clarified the limits of human knowledge in his *Critique of Pure Reason*. However, he then argued that human thought moves beyond these limits in thinking about God, freedom, and immortality. Kant believed that he had set the limits of knowledge in order to make room for faith. Arendt believes that instead he pointed to the importance of thinking for human existence and to the ability of every person to think beyond the limits of established knowledge.

While Arendt maintains that thinking belongs to everyone, not just a few philosophers, she also emphasizes that thinking does not result in further knowledge. Rather, thinking is a quest for meaning. The quest for meaning does not serve the end of knowledge and is not "guided by practical pursuits." The quest for meaning is on going and does not rest in any final results. Indeed, thinking is suspicious of fixed understandings of good and evil. Arendt says that thinking, which is a quest for meaning, is constantly unraveling. Moreover, thinking is about the intangible, about that which is not present, and so serves to remove humans from the world rather than helping to build an on-going world.

Arendt makes use of the analogy of Penelope as she wrestles with the justification for thinking about thinking. Penelope was the wife of Odysseus, the Greek hero. Odysseus left her to care for his large holdings while he went to fight the Trojan War. After ten years of fighting, he began the journey home, which took another ten years. When it began to appear that Odysseus would not return, suitors began to attempt to convince Penelope that he was dead and that it was time for her to remarry. They, of course, wanted Odysseus' property. She postponed them by weaving a tapestry and promising to decide whom she would marry when the tapestry was completed. Each night she undid what she had woven during the day. This continued until Odysseus returned.

While Arendt does not develop the analogy, it helps her wrestle with the issue of whether or not she should dare to think about thinking. Penelope remained true to Odysseus through her action, even if she created nothing tangible in the world. Yet, Penelope's actions were not irrelevant. Arendt raises the question about thinking, "How can anything relevant for the world we live in arise out of so resultless an enterprise?" Convinced that this is a question worth pursuing, she suggests that the only way to think about this question is to trace experiences of thinking.

Socrates as the Representative of Thinking

Arendt emphasizes that she wants to trace the experience of thinking. She maintains that thinking is a faculty that can be ascribed to everyone. In order to trace the experience of thinking, she identifies a representative of "everybody." She selects Socrates because he "did think without becoming a philosopher" (427). More importantly, she believes that Socrates is able to represent everyone because "he possessed a representative significance in reality which only needed some purification in order to reveal its full meaning" (428). Socrates is a real person, not an abstract idea. Arendt believes that his life as transmitted historically, especially through Plato, presents humans with an ideal type of the person who thinks.

In tracing the experience of thinking using Socrates as the model or representative, Arendt notes that Socrates constantly asks questions to which he admits he does not know the answers. This keeps his thought in motion. His thinking moves to and fro, following the directions opened by the questions. Socrates asks about everyday concepts. Indeed, Aristotle identifies Socrates as the person who discovered concepts. He asks about happiness, courage, and justice. Arendt says of these concepts,

> *These words, used to group together seen and manifest qualities and occurrences but nevertheless relating to something unseen, are part and parcel of our everyday speech, and still we can give no account of them; when we try to define them, they get slippery; when we talk about their meaning, nothing stays put anymore, everything begins to move.* (429)

She notes that in meditating on concepts, humans "unfreeze" or "defrost" them (431). Using the example of the concept 'house,' Arendt suggests that someone who meditates on the concept of a house might take better care of his or her own dwelling. But she also notes that this also may not happen. Socrates' way of asking questions and exploring concepts may reveal something about the relation of thinking and doing, but Arendt acknowledges that it is not so simple as meditating on a concept and deriving definitions to direct conduct.

Arendt does, however, believe that Socrates held that talking and thinking about concepts could have an impact on people. Talking and thinking about justice can lead people to act more justly. If this is the case, then thinking should help us avoid becoming evil. She continues to struggle with the connection of thinking and doing by looking at three similes used to describe Socrates. She notes that he called himself a gadfly and a midwife, and that he was also called an electric ray. She believes that these similes help disclose the complicated connection between thinking and doing.

As a gadfly, Socrates aroused the citizens of Athens to self-examination, to thinking about those things that make life most fully human. As a midwife, Socrates identifies himself as "sterile," since midwives in Athens were beyond childbearing age. Moreover, a midwife helps others give birth. Socrates helped others give birth to their thoughts. In addition, the midwife in Athens decided whether the child that was born was fit to live or was a "windegg" and so requiring purging, abortion. Arendt believes that Socrates functioned as a midwife primarily in this purging capacity. He helped people get rid of bad opinions. She says, "he purged people of their...unexamined prejudgments which prevent thinking by suggesting that we know where we not only don't know but cannot know" (432). The electric ray stings and paralyzes. Arendt maintains that Socrates is not content to arouse and purge thought. He also paralyzes.

Arendt interprets this paralysis as an important moment in thinking. It does not mean that the thinker ceases to think. However, thinking does have "an undermining effect on all established criteria, values, measurements for good and evil, in short on those customs and rules of conduct we treat of in morals and ethics" (434). Thinking makes us stop, and so interrupts all other activities. There is no guarantee that those activities will resume or that they will be guided by anything better that the values that have been undermined. Arendt notes that some of the young men who followed Socrates turned to license and cynicism. She concludes, "Thinking is equally dangerous to all creeds and, by itself, does not bring forth any new creed" (435).

Arendt cautions that the inability of thinking to improve people does not mean that it is better to be unthinking. She returns to the events of Nazi Germany and notes that when people do not think, it is much easier to get them to reverse their behavior. It was easy in Germany to reverse the commandment not to kill.

Still struggling to discover whether thinking can help people resist evil, Arendt notes that Socrates speaks of his quest for meaning as *erôs*, as a love that is a need or desire for what it does not have. She combines this understanding of the quest with his additional insight that consciousness is split. Each person is two, able to be conscious of itself. This division is in accord with Arendt's understanding of plurality as fundamental to a fully human world. However, if the fundamental dialogue of thinking takes place within each person, then it is important to see that "the two who carry on the thinking dialogue be in good shape, that the partners be friends" (442). This is why Socrates claims that it is better to be wronged than to do wrong. It is much easier to remain the friend of one who is wronged than of a wrong doer. Arendt uses the example of Shakespeare's Richard III to illustrate this claim. After he has committed many crimes, his dialogue with himself leads him to acknowledge that he hates himself.

With Socrates as the representative of thinking, Arendt concludes that thinking does society very little good most of the time. It challenges values rather than creating them and it moves people to engage in dialogue with themselves rather than create something of permanence. Yet, she believes that at those historical moments when, as Yeats wrote, "Things fall apart; the centre cannot hold," thinking has political importance. Thinkers who have become friends with themselves will not betray themselves and so will not betray others.

She notes that what these people have developed is the faculty of judgment. They can "judge particulars without subsuming them under general rules" (446). This judging follows the insight of experience, rather than rules. It is the ability to tell right from wrong. Arendt says that judging is not the same as thinking, but it is a by-product of thinking.

Arendt uses Socrates as the representative of everyone to trace the experience of thinking and its implications for judging good and evil. However, she also had other guides. Her experience has also been her guide, her model. In the dark times in which she lived, she noted that those who had been aroused, who had purged themselves of unfounded prejudgments, and who had been paralyzed by thought and so been directed to befriend themselves were most able to judge well and so resist the forces of evil.

The Life of the Mind

In June of 1972, Arendt was invited to give the Gifford Lectures at the University of Aberdeen in Scotland. She took this as the opportunity to complete the philosophical work that she had begun when she wrote *The Human Condition*. In *The Human Condition*, she focuses on the *vita activa*, the active life. The Gifford Lectures were intended to result in a book that focuses on the *vita contemplativa*, the contemplative life. Arendt divided the lectures into three parts, thinking, willing, and judging. She proposed that the first two parts would constitute the major portion of the lectures and the resulting book. "Judging" was to be a shorter final section. Arendt delivered the first part, "Thinking" in the Spring of 1973. She was to give the lectures on "Willing" in the Spring of 1974. However, after the first lecture she suffered a heart attack and was never able to finish the series. She did present most of the lectures in some form to students at the New School for Social Research. After her death, her friend and literary executor, Mary McCarthy, edited the lectures and facilitated their publication in the two volumes titled *The Life of the Mind*. The first volume contains the lectures on "Thinking." The second volume presents the work on "Willing" and includes an appendix with material from lectures on Kant's political philosophy that Arendt probably would have used in formulating the section on judging.

In the lectures, Arendt addresses all of the issues that give focus to her life's thought. She wants to think about thinking without becoming trapped in metaphysics and so she ponders how to think about thinking without fleeing from the realities of mortal existence. She wants to ask if it is possible for thinking to prevent humans from doing evil, and so she consults the history of philosophy for ways to think about willing and judging that will help her address this question. The lectures also provide Arendt with the opportunity to present her thought in its unity. Because so many of her works were stimulated by and in response to political events, there is no one place where the insights are presented together in a way to take on unified form. Yet, like Penelope, she is reluctant to complete her project by giving it a final and finished form.

Indeed, Arendt notes that she does not have a method to present. She claims that her project is really concerned with dismantling. We live in a period in which the thread of tradition is broken. There is no on-going unity with the past. Dismantling is a process that involves dealing with a fragmented past. Arendt does not suggest that the fragments can be put back together in some new and unified whole. Indeed, she cautions those who might also try this dismantling to "be careful not to destroy the 'rich and strange,' the 'coral' and the 'pearl,' which can probably be saved only as fragments" (I, 212). Her caution is clearly influenced by Benjamin's work.

Yet, Arendt does place the fragments together in a sort of order. If we live with fragments, we still construct a meaningful world making use of the fragments. We do this in the span that we have between birth and death, in what Arendt calls the gap between past and future. She writes,

The gap...is...the path paved by thinking, the small inconspicuous track of non-time beaten by the activity of thought within the time-space given to natal and mortal men. Following that course, the thought-trains, remembrance and anticipation, save whatever they touch from the ruin of historical and biographical time. (I, 210)

The two volumes that result from the Gifford Lectures pull together many of the thought-trains that Arendt discovered and saved in the course of her time between birth and death. They are rich with provocative insights and sometimes confusing complexities.

In the first volume on "Thinking," Arendt develops the issues that she outlined in the lecture on "Thinking and Moral Considerations." She situates the conclusions about thinking that she presented in that lecture by identifying the three mental activities of thinking, willing, and judging. She maintains that each of these activities is basic. They cannot be reduced to some common denominator. Each is autonomous, obeying "the laws inherent in the activity itself" (I, 70). While she maintains that there is no hierarchy of these three activities, she does suggest that thinking prepares the mind for the other two activities. Because of this, it is appropriate to think about the activity of thinking before taking up willing and judging.

Arendt also presents these three activities of the mind as revealing the temporal structure and the freedom of contingent humanity. Thinking is the activity of the mind that is most concerned with the past. It gathers the fragments that can be used to create meaning. It is in many respects a spectator activity. However, this very ability to draw back protects the freedom of the mind. Willing is the activity most concerned with the future. Willing directs human life towards an end. While philosophers have often taken this to mean that humans are defined by death or live in preparation for death, Arendt reiterates the importance of birth, of natality, for understanding our temporal structure. She calls on her early work on Augustine who emphasizes that God created humans as temporal creatures. She describes each birth as "the entry of a novel creature who *as* something entirely new appears in the midst of the time continuum of the world" (II, 217). The activity of willing is concerned with acting upon the possibilities of each individual new beginning. Judging is the most worldly of the activities of the mind and so most corresponds to the present and to the world in which we actually live. In the activity of judging, we deal with the particularities of our lives. Willing and judging both seem to require an actual realm of political freedom for speaking and acting. When that realm is diminished or does not exist, thinking preserves freedom and protects the fragments that may again be brought forward to help construct a political realm for the thriving of human plurality and diversity.

The incompleteness of *The Life of the Mind* leaves the contemporary reader and thinker with the challenge of reflecting on judging in the context of the fragments of the past and the hope for the future that Arendt presents. Perhaps it is appropriate that she died before the books were completed. She was never tempted to give her thought a final form. It is difficult to be an Arendtian in the way that one can be a Thomist or a Hegelian. Instead of a school of thought, Arendt left to us the challenge to continue to think what we are doing, even when we are thinking.

8
Arendt and Contemporary Thought

Hannah Arendt's thought provokes questions more than it provides answers. Her work presents intriguing concepts, such as the concept of natality, that call for further reflection and development. While most thinkers find parts of her work problematic or lacking clarity, the richness of her thinking has provided the wide-ranging impetus for further thought. Larry May and Jerome Kohn note in the Introduction to *Hannah Arendt: Twenty Years Later*, that in wrestling with the practical and theoretical issues that concerned Arendt, writers

> *frequently employ terms of discourse other than hers, but Arendt would not have objected to that. In fact, she would not have wanted it any other way, for her own mode of thinking simply and consistently precludes anything that even remotely resembled discipleship.* (6)

For those who are influenced by her work, often the example of Arendt as a thinker is as important as the specifics of her thought. However, aspects of Arendt's thought have continued to illuminate issues of importance to philosophical thought and political and social life as the human world begins a new century.

Philosophical Influences

Trying to understand an author often involves understanding the influences that have contributed to that author's thinking. Some of the contemporary work related to Arendt's thought has taken this direction. Two philosophical influences are of particular interest, Augustine and Heidegger.

Arendt wrote her doctoral dissertation on Augustine and love. The question quickly presents itself: Why would a young Jewish woman in Germany write on an early Christian thinker? While the psychological answer to such a question may never be found, the philosophical influences of this choice can be traced. Elisabeth Young-Bruehl emphasizes the importance of the work on Augustine in choosing "For Love of the World" as the subtitle of her biography of Arendt. Others, such as Ronald Beiner, argue that in this early work "Arendt was a political philosopher before she knew that she was one" (May 270). Both believe that the work on Augustine is extremely important for understanding the questions that Arendt raises.

Her relationship to Heidegger is more complicated. A German edition of some of their correspondence is now available for those who are interested in the love affair between them. The more philosophically interesting questions, however, have to do with the influences of Heidegger's thought on Arendt. The two took very different political directions, yet anyone who reads Arendt who has also read Heidegger is struck by how much she owes him. He introduced her to the phenomenological method that she develops. Many of the issues and concepts that she finds important first appear in Heidegger's thought. Even the concept of natality is there in Heidegger waiting to be developed. There is much work left to be done to show both how Arendt is indebted to Heidegger and how her work provides the directions for a critique of his thinking, particularly in regards to the political.

The Political

Most of the thinking that has been inspired by Arendt's work has addressed questions about the political. Arendt's distinction between the private and the public is problematic. It confines household activities to the private realm and so makes it difficult to explore what is political in the private. It places the social in a strange middle position that separates it from the political in ways that are not really true to experience. However, the distinction also contributes to an understanding of the need for a public space in which humans can meet and speak freely about a wide range of issues.

Arendt's work has inspired further reflections on totalitarianism and bureaucracy, on specific political situations and how to understand these situations, and on questions about political structure. It has led people to ask about the relationship of economics and freedom. Perhaps most importantly, her thought has contributed to rethinking the relationship of meaning of concepts such as authority, power, and force. All of this thought contributes to the vitality of a free human community and so continues the task that Arendt found so important for human existence.

The Ethical

The most important ethical question raised by Arendt is the question of the nature of evil. Questions about the origin and impact of evil give shape to much of her thought, particularly after the Eichmann trial. These and similar questions continue to be raised by those influenced by Arendt's thought.

However, Arendt's work raises many other serious ethical questions. If her analysis is correct, then ethics is not best characterized or developed as a practice of following rules or principles. Rather, ethics has to do with thinking and acting in particular situations out of an understanding of experience and a hope for the future. Her ethics is influenced by existentialism. Yet, it recognizes the importance of common sense. While some work has been done on her ethical thought, there is more to be done, particularly in relationship to current work in feminist ethics.

The Social

One of Arendt's most problematic concepts is "the social." Much of the rest of her philosophical analysis seems to fit human experience. When she talks about language and clichés and the dangers they present to human life, it is easy to identify examples from experience. However, Arendt's treatment of the social does not ring so true.

Hanna Pitkin says, "the concept was confused and her way of deploying it radically at odds with her most central and valuable teaching" (1). Pitkin calls Arendt's concept of the social, the "Blob." She believes that Arendt's thinking shows the need to rethink the social in order to find ways of moving what Arendt termed the political into the social. Pitkin maintains that Arendt's work challenges people to find ways of transforming the social so that its blob-like characteristics cannot prevail. Pitkin also maintains that Arendt's thought provides one of the main directions for attempting such transformation. Arendt's emphasis on the human ability to begin provides Pitkin with hope. Pitkin says,

> *Once we do begin, moreover, we may find others already under way, may discover all sorts of organizations and movements – be they about ecology, feminism, disarmament, torture, human rights, or nuclear power – movements locally generated but aimed at public responsibility and power.* (283).

Pitkin agrees with Hans Jonas who noted at Arendt's funeral that even her errors were worthwhile. Her problematic account of the social has pushed others to think about the role of the social in relation to human freedom.

Feminist Interpretations

Hannah Arendt was not a feminist. While she came to see the importance of claiming her identity as a Jew, she never recognized the same significance for her identity as a woman. She believed that the feminist movement that emerged in the 1960s and 1970s was unneeded and ideological. Yet, aspects of her thought are in agreement with various feminist approaches. Her concern with an ethics that begins with rules is confirmed and addressed by feminist ethics. Her insight into the importance of beginning with experience rather than theory is also shared by contemporary feminism.

Even if Arendt did not want to identify herself with feminism, her thought has contributed to contemporary feminist work. Feminist thought has profited from her concept of natality. It has critiqued her positioning of the role of housework and of the gender roles implied in

87

her distinction between labor and work, which identifies labor with the feminine and work with the masculine. Arendt's emphasis on the importance of metaphor and narrative also contribute to contemporary feminist thought. Bonnie Honig, the editor of Feminist *Interpretations of Hannah Arendt*, remarks that the result of feminist thinking out of Arendt's work "is a startling plurality of findings and judgments, a diverse array of feminist theories and practices, and a Hannah Arendt who, while not herself a feminist, emerges as a vital and reinvigorating thinker for feminists to engage" (14). If Arendt had lived to observe more of the contemporary feminist movement, perhaps she would have welcomed the diversity of perspectives that it endorses and embodies.

Sustaining the Tentative

Arendt's writing provides many possibilities for contemporary thought. At the 1972 conference in Toronto, Arendt reflected on her own work and on her conversations with Jaspers. She said,

> *I would like to say that everything I did and everything I wrote – all that is tentative. I think that all thinking, the way that I have indulged in it perhaps a little beyond measure, extravagantly, has the earmark of being tentative. And what was so great in these conversations with Jaspers was that you could sustain an effort, which was merely tentative, which did not aim at any results, for weeks.* (Hill 338)

Arendt's work continues to contribute to conversations that sustain the tentative and so her work continues to contribute to the contemporary task of building and preserving a more human world.

Chronology

1906	Hannah Arendt born, Hanover Germany
1910	Move to Königsberg
1913	Death of her father and grandfather
1920	Remarriage of her mother to Martin Beerwald
1924	Moves to Marburg to attend university
1925	Begins work with Jaspers at Heidelberg
1929	Marries Günther Stern
1933	Leaves Germany and settles in France
1939	Divorce from Günther Stern finalized
1940	Marries Heinrich Blücher
1941	Immigrates to the United States
1951	*Origins of Totalitarianism* published
1958	*The Human Condition* published
1958	*Rachel Varnhagen: The Life of a Jewish Woman* published
1961	*Between Past and Future* published
1963	*Eichmann in Jerusalem* published
1963	*On Revolution* published
1968	*Men in Dark Times* published
1968	Revised edition of *Between Past and Future* published
1970	*On Violence* published
1970	Heinrich Blücher dies
1972	*Crises of the Republic* published
1975	Hannah Arendt dies
1978	*The Life of the Mind* (two volumes of the uncompleted work) published
1978	*The Jew as Pariah: Jewish Identity and the Politics of the Modern Age* published
1982	*Lectures on Kant's Political Philosophy* published

Bibliography

Selected Works in English by Hannah Arendt

Between Friends, The Correspondence of Hannah Arendt and Mary McCarthy. Ed. Carol Brightman. New York: Harcourt Brace & Company, 1995.

Between Past and Future: Six Exercises in Political Thought. New York, Viking Press, 1961. Revised edition, including two additional essays, 1968.

Crises of the Republic. New York: Harcourt Brace & Company, 1972.

Eichmann in Jerusalem. New York: Penguin Books, 1994.

Hannah Arendt – Karl Jaspers Correspondence, 1929-1969. Ed. Lotte Kohler and Hans Saner. Trans. Robert and Rita Kimber. New York: Harcourt Brace Jovanovich, 1992.

The Human Condition. Second Edition with Introduction by Margaret Canovan. Chicago: The University of Chicago Press, 1998.

The Life of the Mind, two volumes. New York: Harcourt Brace Jovanovich, 1978.

Love and Saint Augustine. Ed. Joanna Vecchiarelli Scott and Judith Chelius Stark. Chicago: University of Chicago Press, 1996.

Men in Dark Times. New York: Harcourt Brace & Company, 1995.

The Origins of Totalitarianism. New York: Harcourt Brace & Company, 1979.

"Thinking and Moral Considerations: A Lecture." *Social Research* 38.3 (Autumn 1971): 417-446.

Selected Works about Hannah Arendt

Bowen-Moore, Patricia. *Hannah Arendt's Philosophy of Natality.* New York: St. Martin's Press, 1989.

Bradshaw, Leah. *Acting and Thinking: The Political Thought of Hannah Arendt.* Toronto: University of Toronto Press, 1989.

Canovan, Margaret. *The Political Thought of Hannah Arendt.* New York: Harcourt Brace Jovanovich, 1974.

Dossa, Shiraz. *The Public Realm and the Public Self, The Political Theory of Hannah Arendt.* Waterloo, Ontario: Wilfred Laurier UP, 1989.

Gottsegen, Michael G. *The Political Thought of Hannah Arendt.* Albany, NY: SUNY Press, 1994.

Hinchman, Lewis P. and Sandra K. Hinchman (Eds). *Hannah Arendt, Critical Essays.* Albany, NY: SUNY Press, 1994.

Hill, Melvyn A. *Hannah Arendt: The Recovery of the Public World.* New York: St Martin's Press, 1979.

Honig, Bonnie (Ed.). *Feminist Interpretations of Hannah Arendt.* University Park, PA: The Pennsylvania State UP, 1995.

Kateb, George. *Hannah Arendt: Politics, Conscience, Evil.* Totowa, NJ: Rowman and Allanheld, 1984.

May, Derwent. *Hannah Arendt.* New York: Penguin, 1986.

May, Larry and Jerome Kohn (Eds.). *Hannah Arendt, Twenty Years Later.* Cambridge, MA: MIT Press, 1996. (Includes an extensive bibliography of writings in English about Hannah Arendt)

Parekh, Bhikhu. *Hannah Arendt and the Search for a New Political Philosophy.* Atlantic Highlands, NJ: Humanities Press, 1981.

Pitkin, Hanna Fenichel. *The Attack of the Blob.* Chicago: University of Chicago Press, 1998.

Ring, Jennifer. *The Political Consequences of Thinking.* Albany, NY: SUNY Press, 1998.

Villa, Dana R. *Arendt and Heidegger: The Fate of the Political.* Princeton, NJ: Princeton UP, 1996.

Young-Bruehl, Elisabeth. *Hannah Arendt, For Love of the World.* New Haven, CT: Yale UP, 1982. (Excellent and extensive biography)